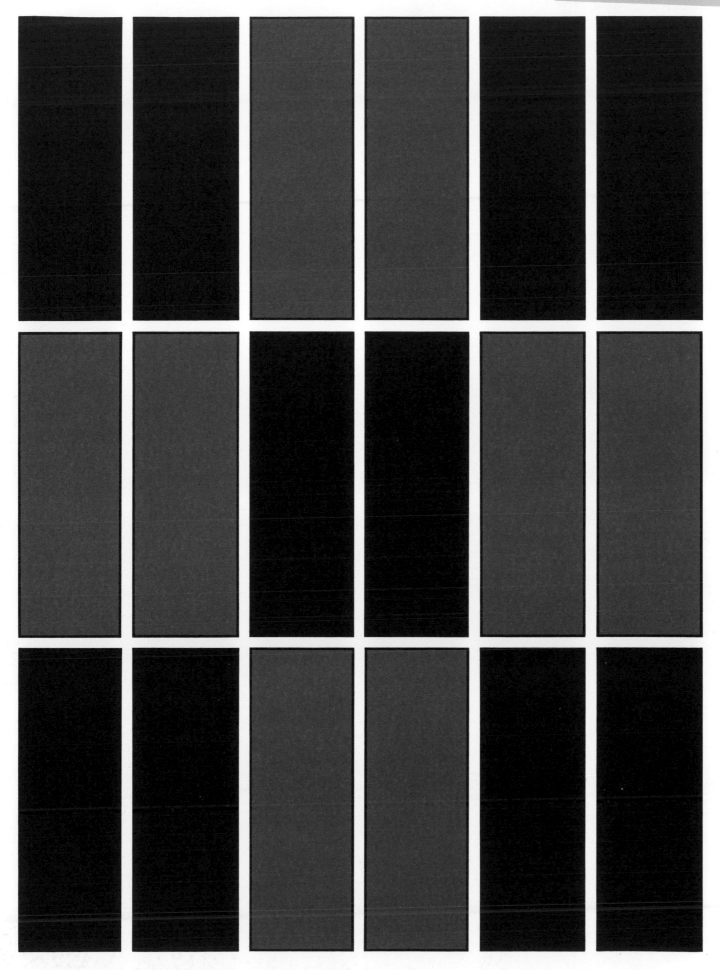

PUBLISHED BY JONATHAN CAPE
2 4 6 8 10 9 7 5 3

FIRST PUBLISHED IN GREAT BRITAIN IN 2010 BY
JONATHAN CAPE
RANDOM HOUSE, 20 VAUXHALL BRIDGE ROAD,
LONDON SW1V 2SA

WWW.RBOOKS.CO.UK

ADDRESSES FOR COMPANIES WITHIN THE RANDOM
HOUSE GROUP LIMITED CAN BE FOUND AT:
WWW.RANDOMHOUSE.CO.UK/OFFICES.HTM

THE RANDOM HOUSE GROUP LIMITED REG. NO. 954009

A CIP CATALOGUE RECORD FOR THIS BOOK IS AVAILABLE
FROM THE BRITISH LIBRARY

ISBN 9780224090414

THE RANDOM HOUSE GROUP LIMITED MAKES EVERY
EFFORT TO ENSURE THAT THE PAPERS USED IN ITS
BOOKS ARE MADE FROM TREES THAT HAVE BEEN LEGALLY
SOURCED FROM WELL-MANAGED AND CREDIBLY CERTIFIED
FORESTS. OUR PAPER PROCUREMENT POLICY CAN BE
FOUND AT: WWW.RANDOMHOUSE.CO.UK/PAPER.HTM

PRINTED IN CHINA

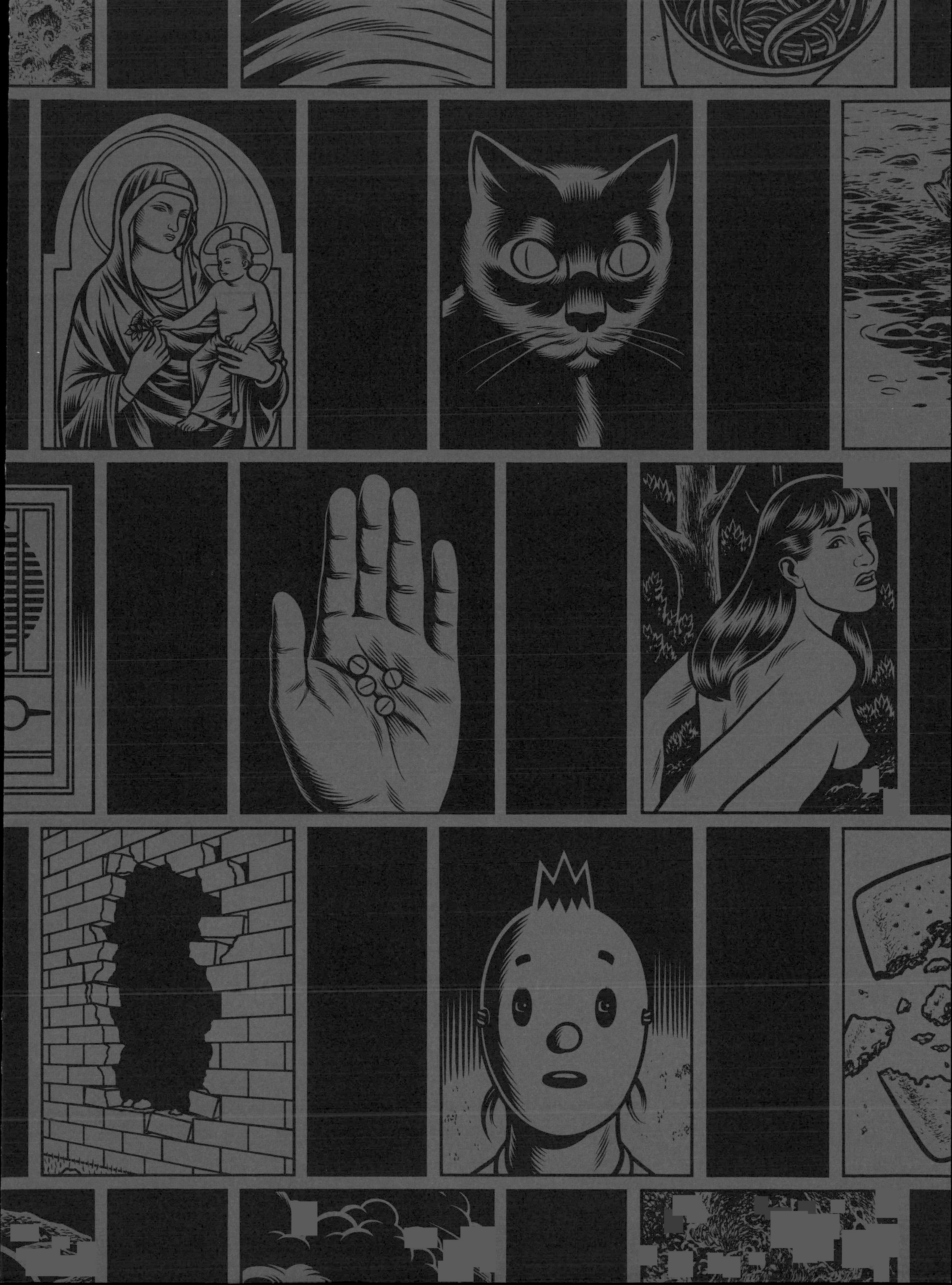

CHARLES BURNS

X'ED OUT

JONATHAN CAPE
LONDON

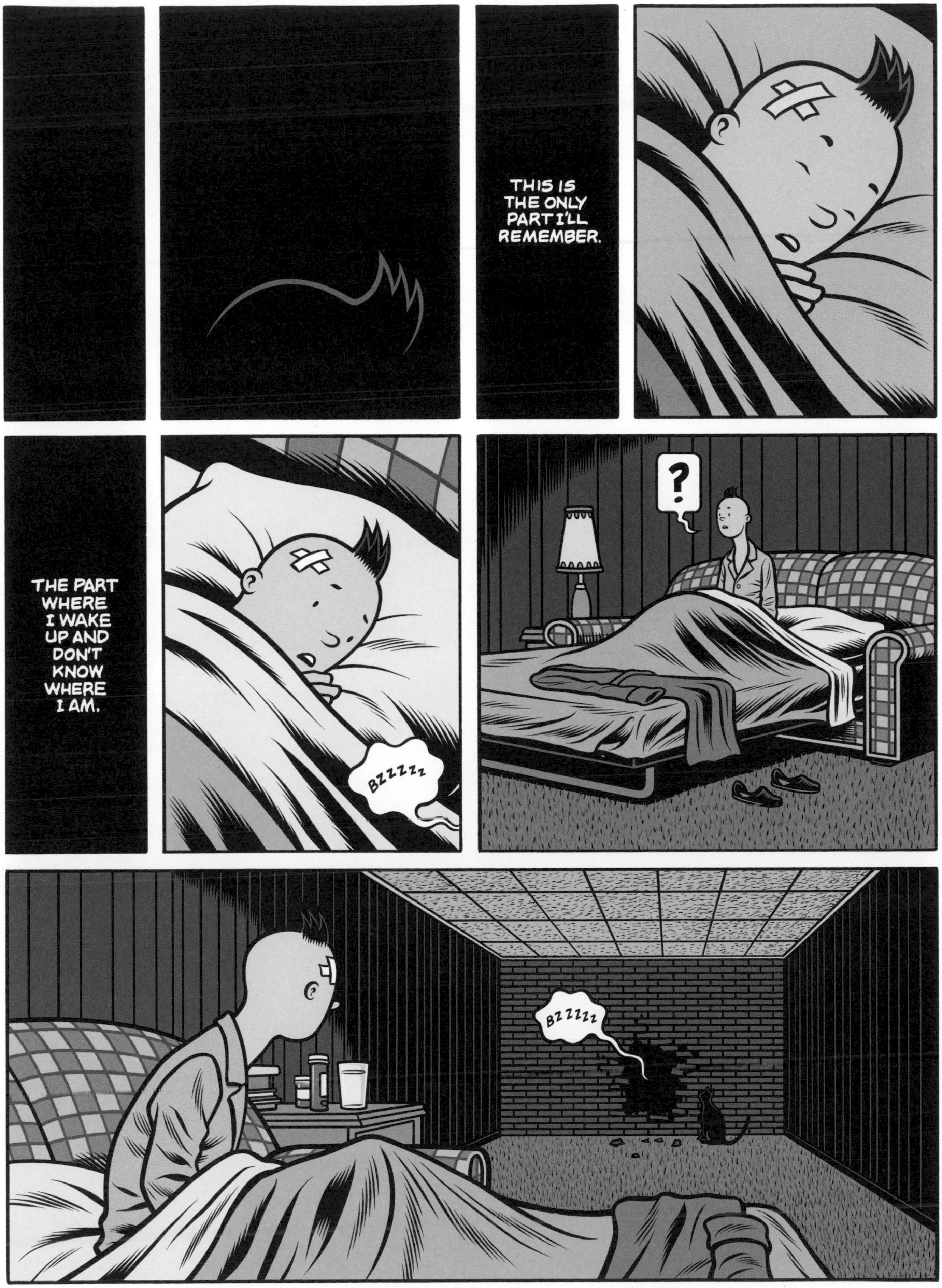
THIS IS THE ONLY PART I'LL REMEMBER.
THE PART WHERE I WAKE UP AND DON'T KNOW WHERE I AM.
BZZZZZ
?
BZZZZZ

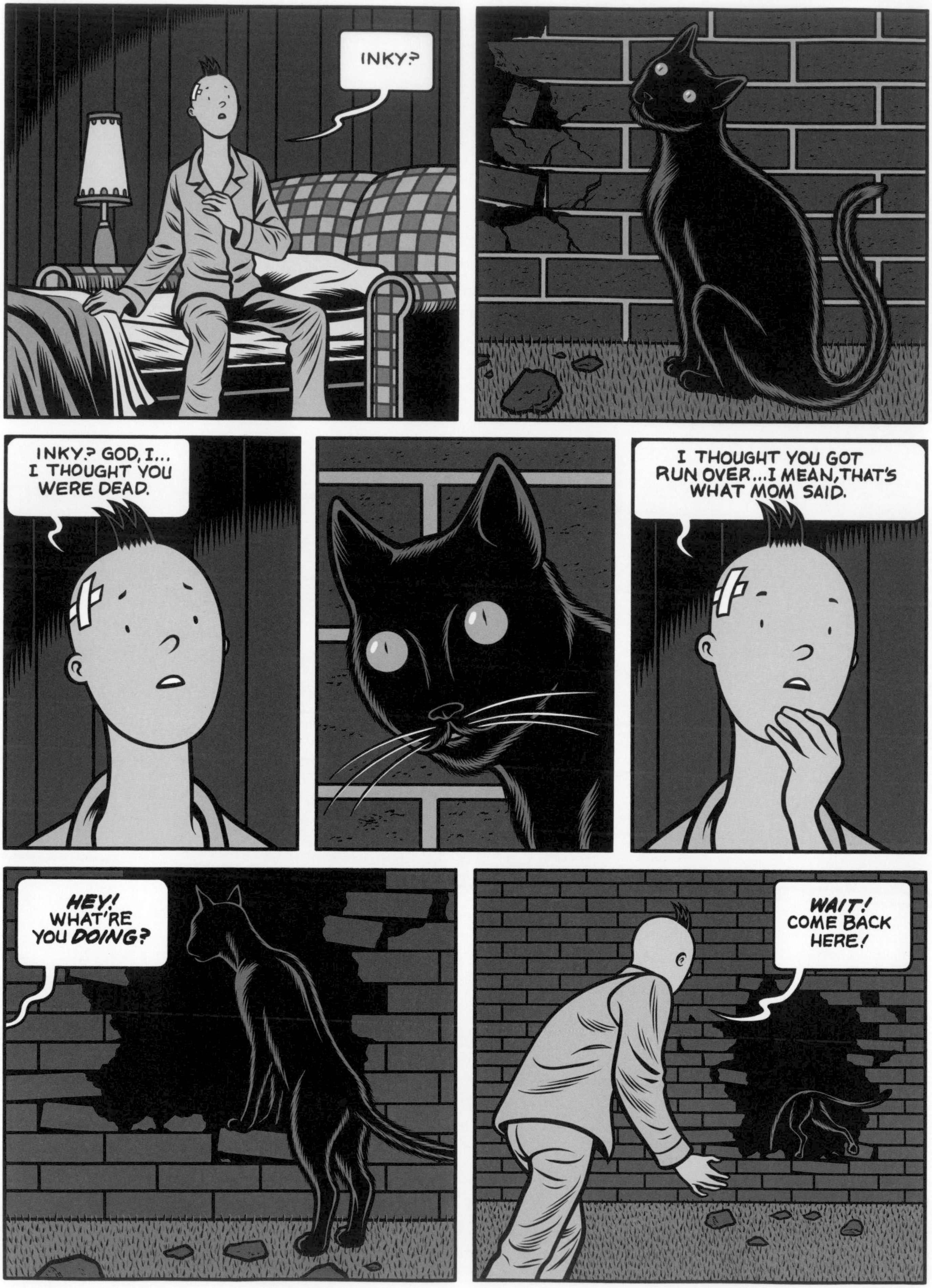
INKY?
INKY? GOD, I... I THOUGHT YOU WERE DEAD.
I THOUGHT YOU GOT RUN OVER...I MEAN, THAT'S WHAT MOM SAID.
HEY! WHAT'RE YOU DOING?
WAIT! COME BACK HERE!

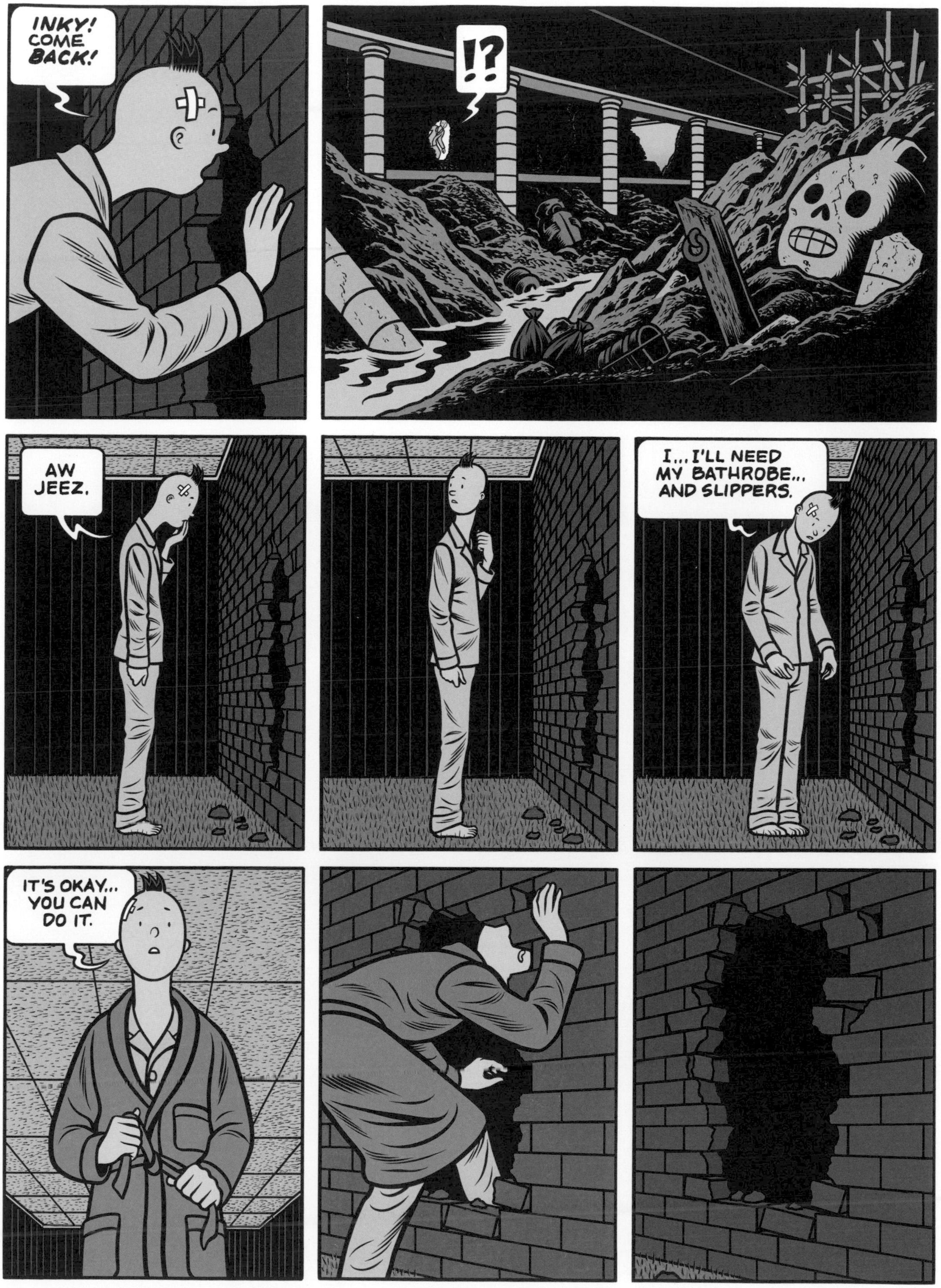
INKY! COME BACK!
!?
AW JEEZ.
I... I'LL NEED MY BATHROBE... AND SLIPPERS.
IT'S OKAY... YOU CAN DO IT.

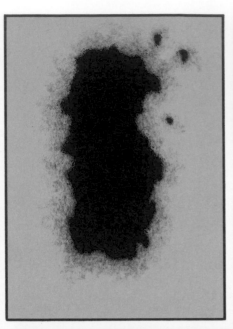

STALE
CIGARETTE
SMOKE...

ICE CUBES
CLINKING
IN A GLASS.

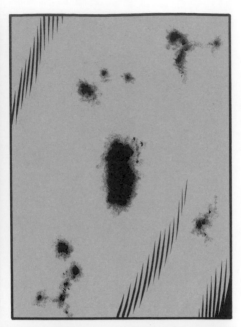

THE FLICKER
OF A DISTANT
TELEVISION...

SOME NEWS
SHOW ABOUT
THE FLOODS...

NUMM?
NUH?

NUMM?
UMMM?

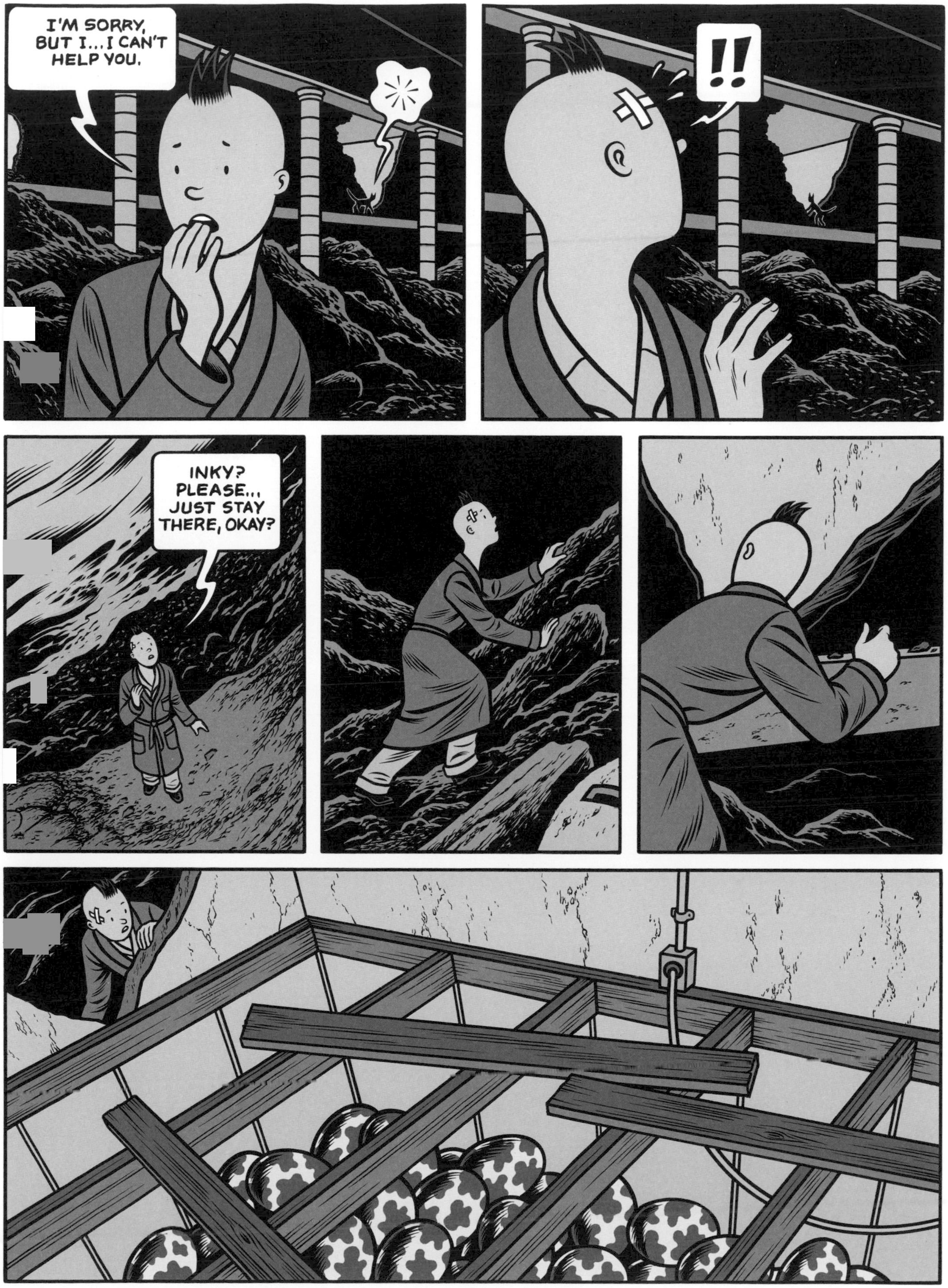
I'M SORRY, BUT I... I CAN'T HELP YOU.
!!
INKY? PLEASE... JUST STAY THERE, OKAY?

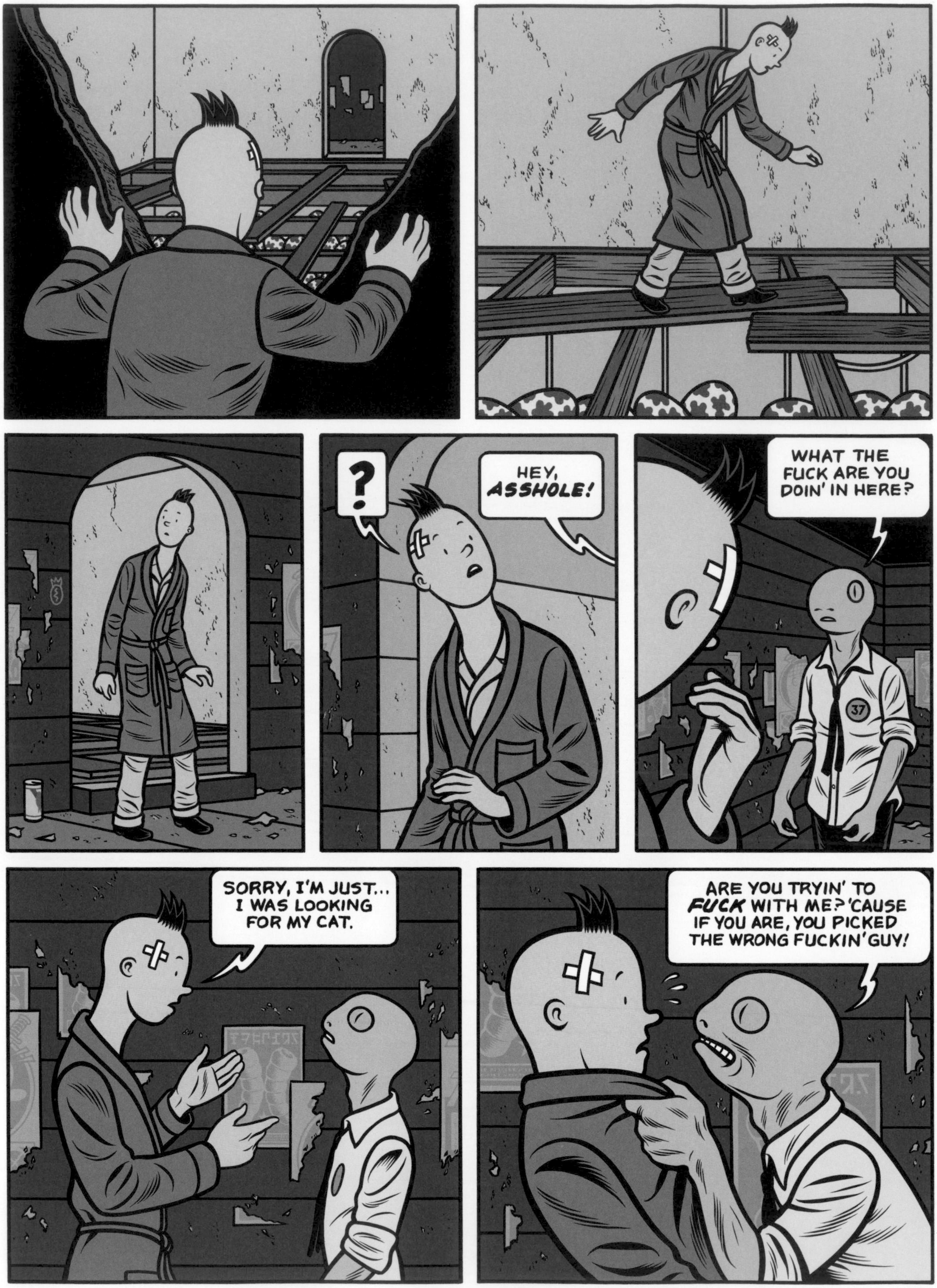
?
HEY, ASSHOLE!
WHAT THE FUCK ARE YOU DOIN' IN HERE?
SORRY, I'M JUST... I WAS LOOKING FOR MY CAT.
ARE YOU TRYIN' TO FUCK WITH ME? 'CAUSE IF YOU ARE, YOU PICKED THE WRONG FUCKIN' GUY!

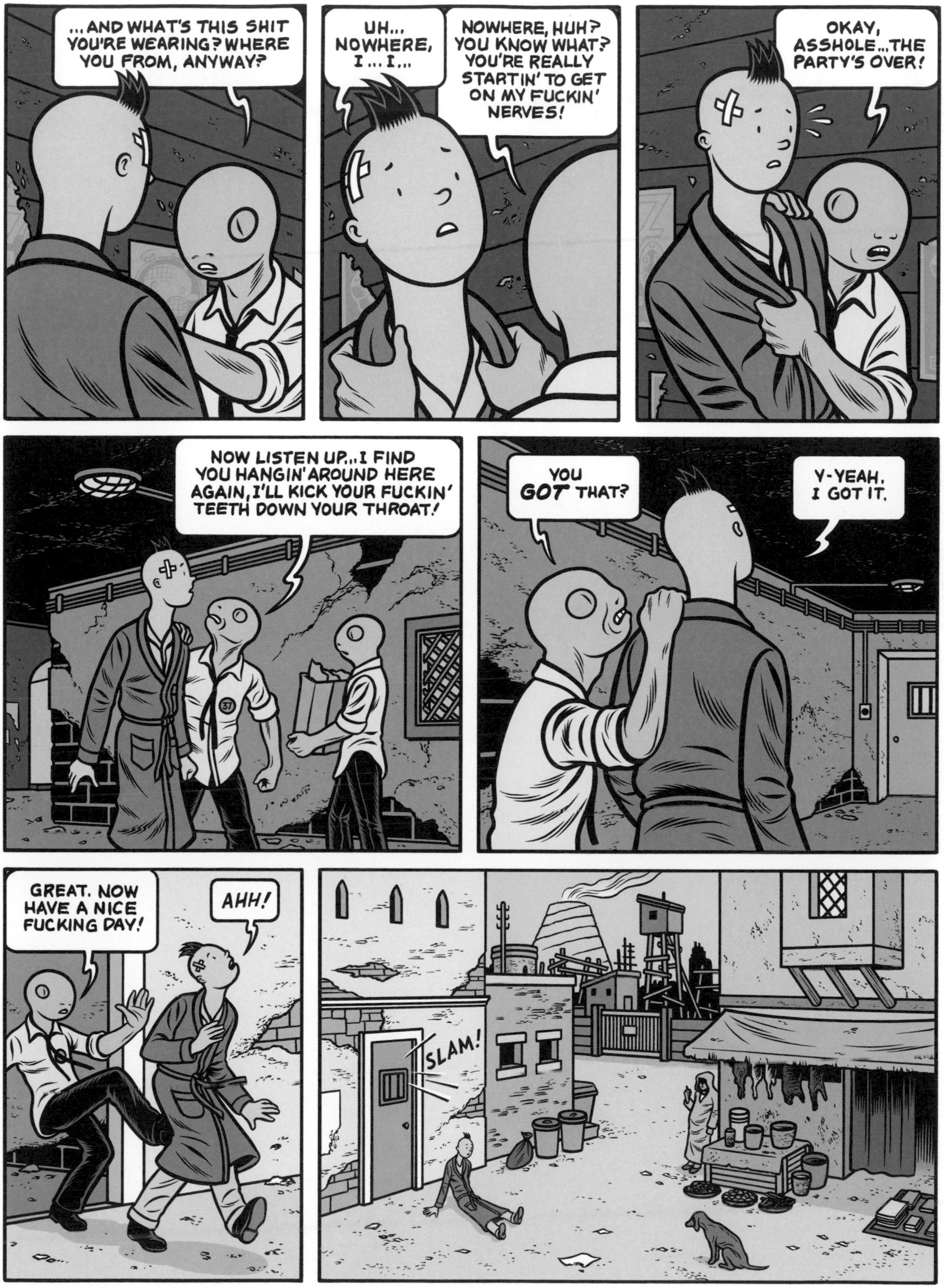
...AND WHAT'S THIS SHIT YOU'RE WEARING? WHERE YOU FROM, ANYWAY?
UH... NOWHERE, I... I...
NOWHERE, HUH? YOU KNOW WHAT? YOU'RE REALLY STARTIN' TO GET ON MY FUCKIN' NERVES!
OKAY, ASSHOLE...THE PARTY'S OVER!
NOW LISTEN UP...I FIND YOU HANGIN' AROUND HERE AGAIN, I'LL KICK YOUR FUCKIN' TEETH DOWN YOUR THROAT!
YOU GOT THAT?
Y-YEAH. I GOT IT.
GREAT. NOW HAVE A NICE FUCKING DAY!
AHH!
SLAM!

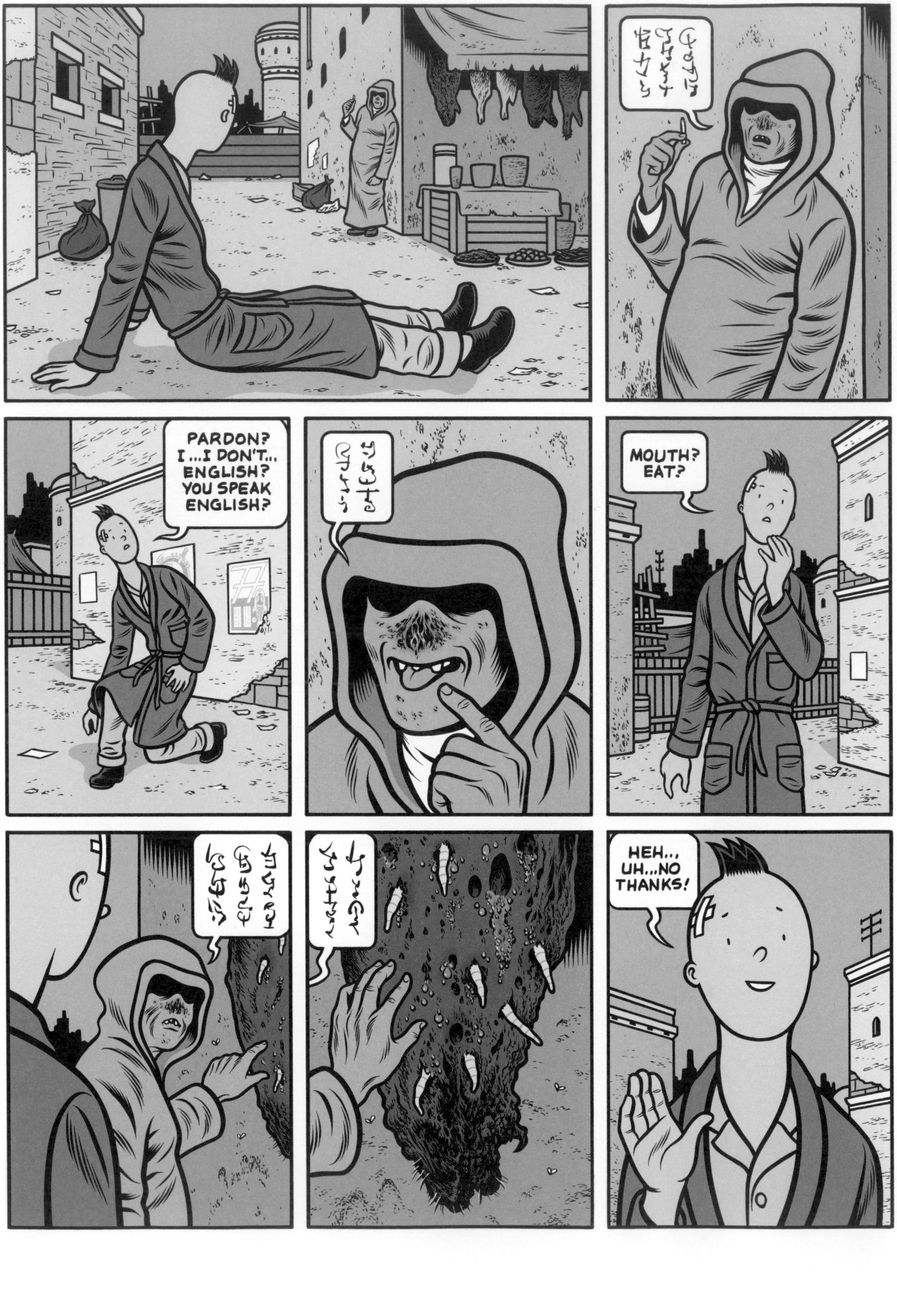
PARDON? I...I DON'T... ENGLISH? YOU SPEAK ENGLISH?
MOUTH? EAT?
HEH.., UH...NO THANKS!

HEY... HEY, MISTER!
YOU DON'T WANNA EAT THAT JUNK... IT'LL MAKE YOU SICK.

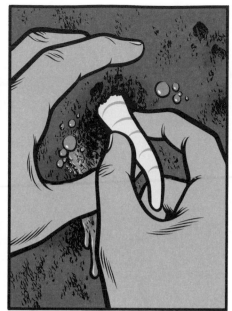

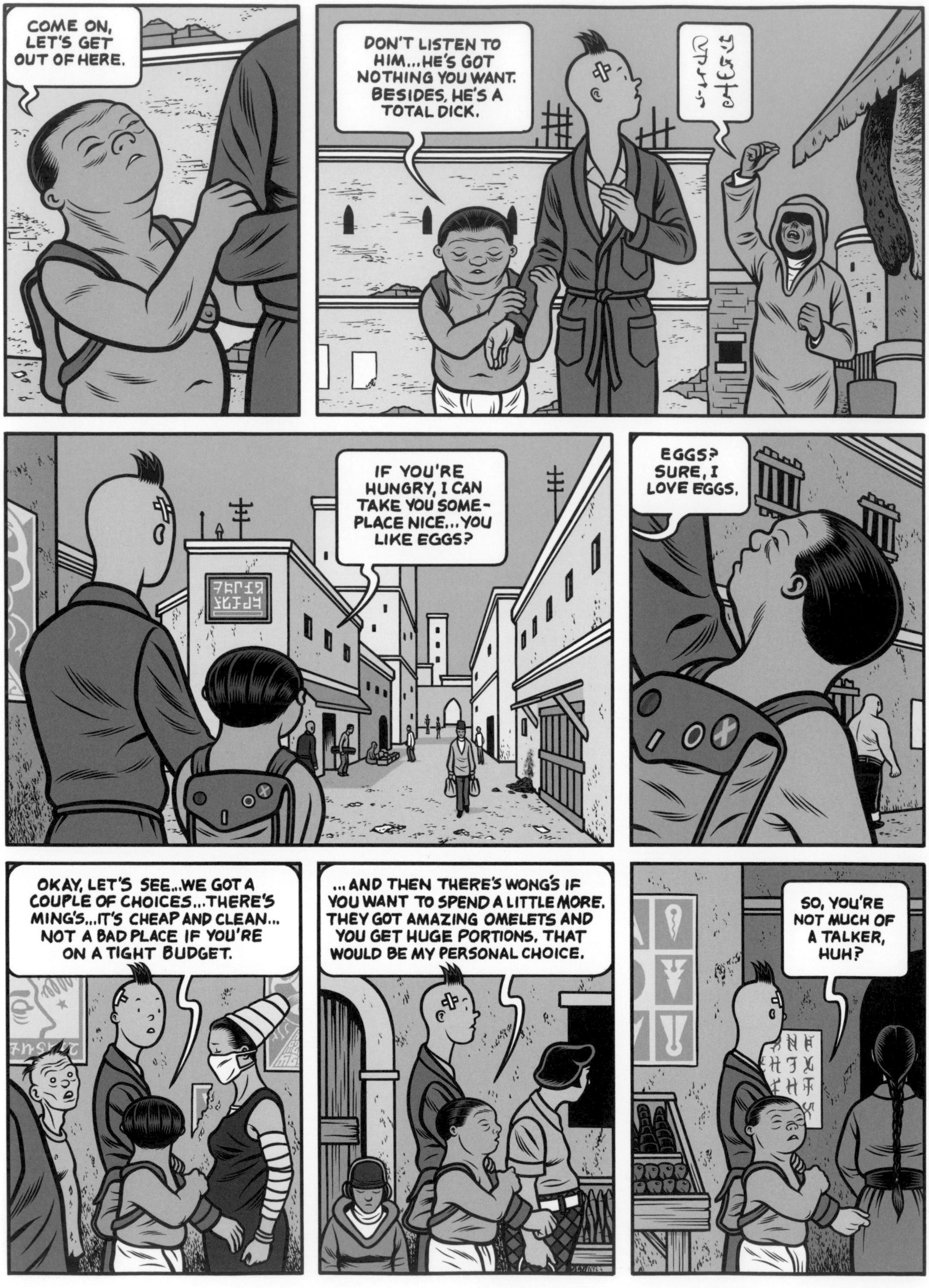

COME ON, LET'S GET OUT OF HERE.
DON'T LISTEN TO HIM... HE'S GOT NOTHING YOU WANT. BESIDES, HE'S A TOTAL DICK.
IF YOU'RE HUNGRY, I CAN TAKE YOU SOME-PLACE NICE... YOU LIKE EGGS?
EGGS? SURE, I LOVE EGGS.
OKAY, LET'S SEE...WE GOT A COUPLE OF CHOICES... THERE'S MING'S...IT'S CHEAP AND CLEAN... NOT A BAD PLACE IF YOU'RE ON A TIGHT BUDGET.
... AND THEN THERE'S WONG'S IF YOU WANT TO SPEND A LITTLE MORE. THEY GOT AMAZING OMELETS AND YOU GET HUGE PORTIONS. THAT WOULD BE MY PERSONAL CHOICE.
SO, YOU'RE NOT MUCH OF A TALKER, HUH?

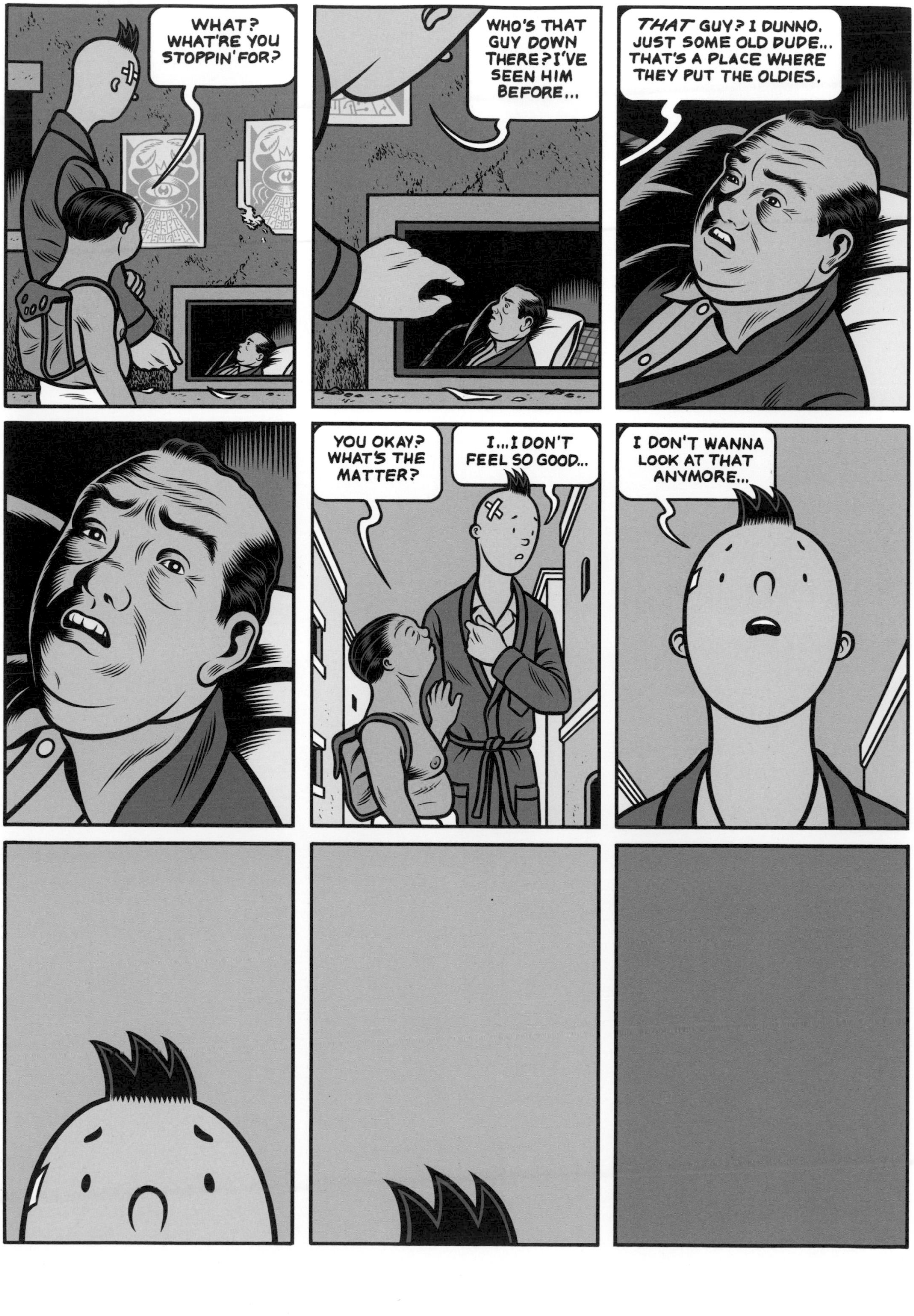
WHAT? WHAT'RE YOU STOPPIN' FOR?
WHO'S THAT GUY DOWN THERE? I'VE SEEN HIM BEFORE...
THAT GUY? I DUNNO. JUST SOME OLD DUDE... THAT'S A PLACE WHERE THEY PUT THE OLDIES.
YOU OKAY? WHAT'S THE MATTER?
I...I DON'T FEEL SO GOOD...
I DON'T WANNA LOOK AT THAT ANYMORE...

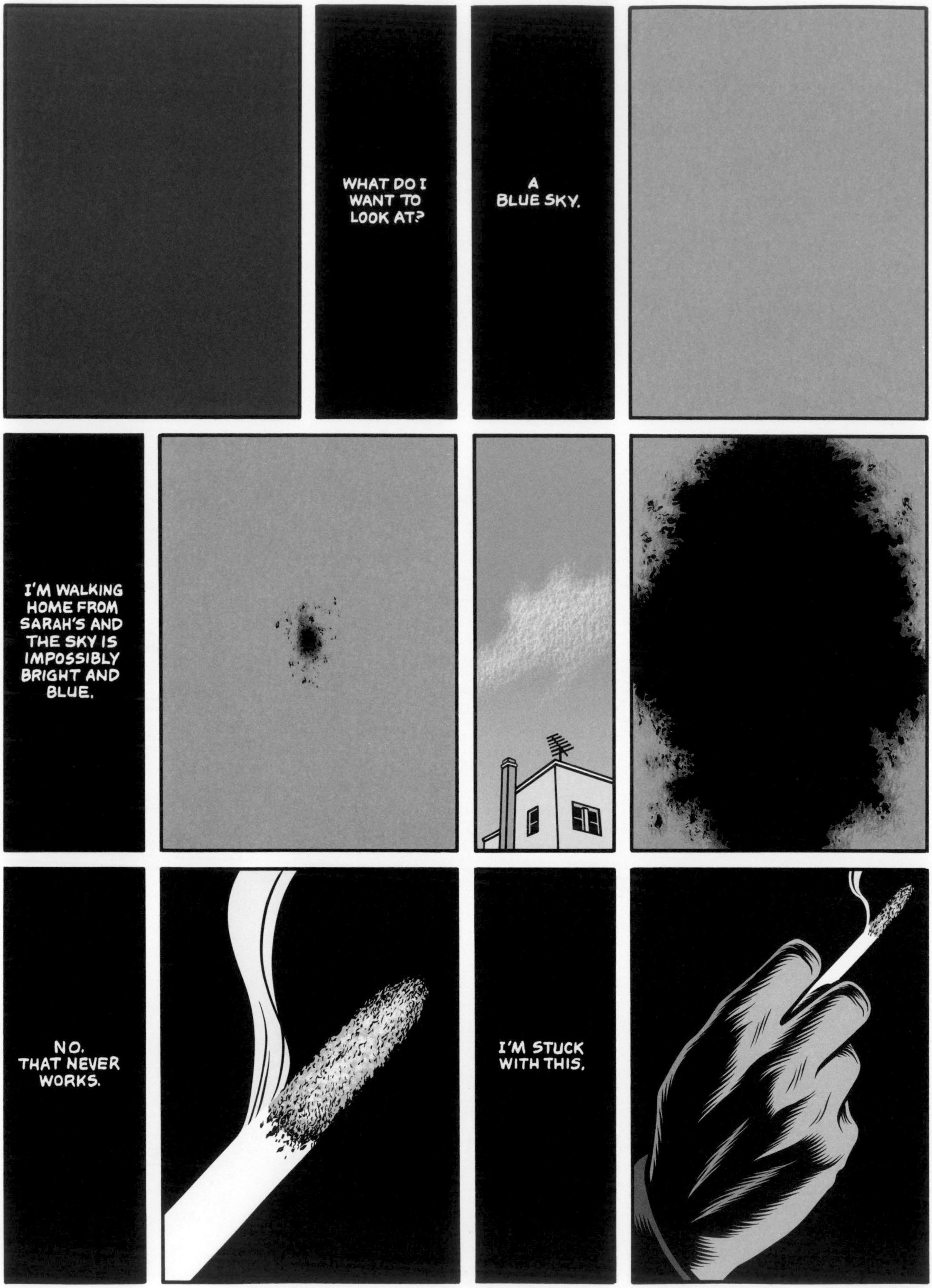
WHAT DO I WANT TO LOOK AT?
A BLUE SKY.
I'M WALKING HOME FROM SARAH'S AND THE SKY IS IMPOSSIBLY BRIGHT AND BLUE.
NO. THAT NEVER WORKS.
I'M STUCK WITH THIS.

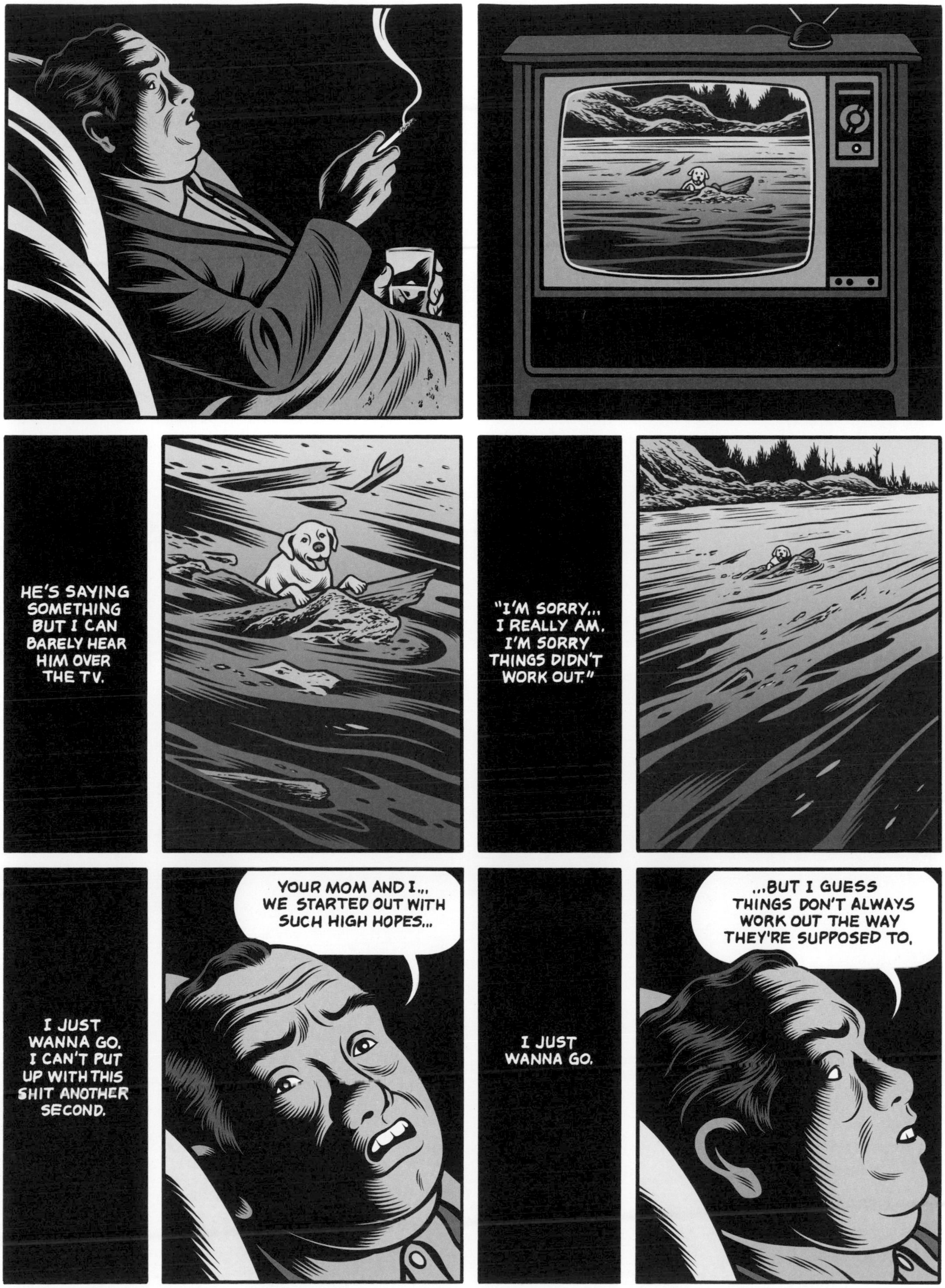
HE'S SAYING SOMETHING BUT I CAN BARELY HEAR HIM OVER THE TV.
"I'M SORRY... I REALLY AM. I'M SORRY THINGS DIDN'T WORK OUT."
I JUST WANNA GO. I CAN'T PUT UP WITH THIS SHIT ANOTHER SECOND.
YOUR MOM AND I... WE STARTED OUT WITH SUCH HIGH HOPES...
I JUST WANNA GO.
...BUT I GUESS THINGS DON'T ALWAYS WORK OUT THE WAY THEY'RE SUPPOSED TO.

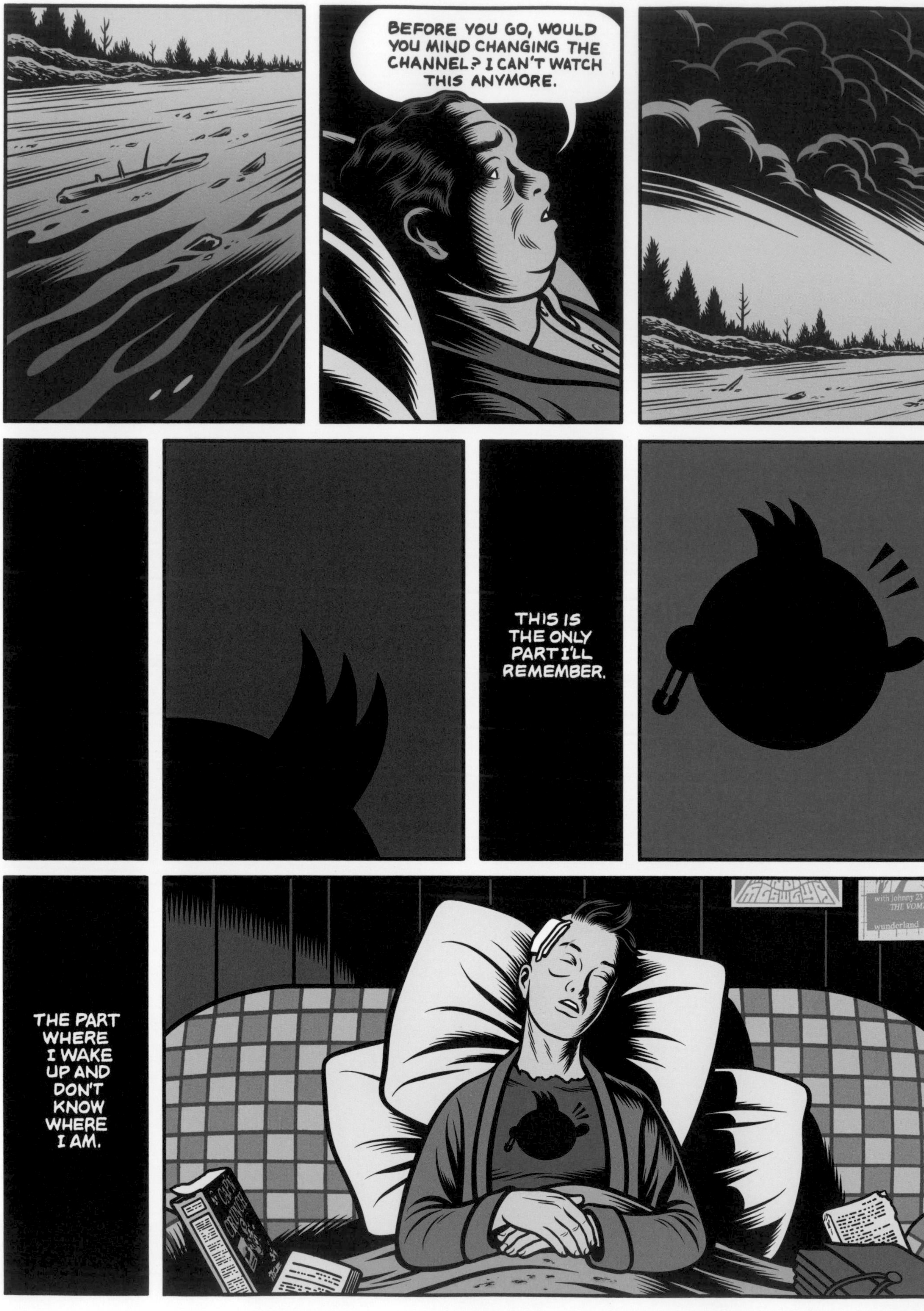
BEFORE YOU GO, WOULD YOU MIND CHANGING THE CHANNEL? I CAN'T WATCH THIS ANYMORE.
THIS IS THE ONLY PART I'LL REMEMBER.
with johnny 23
THE VOMZ
wunderland SEP
THE PART WHERE I WAKE UP AND DON'T KNOW WHERE I AM.

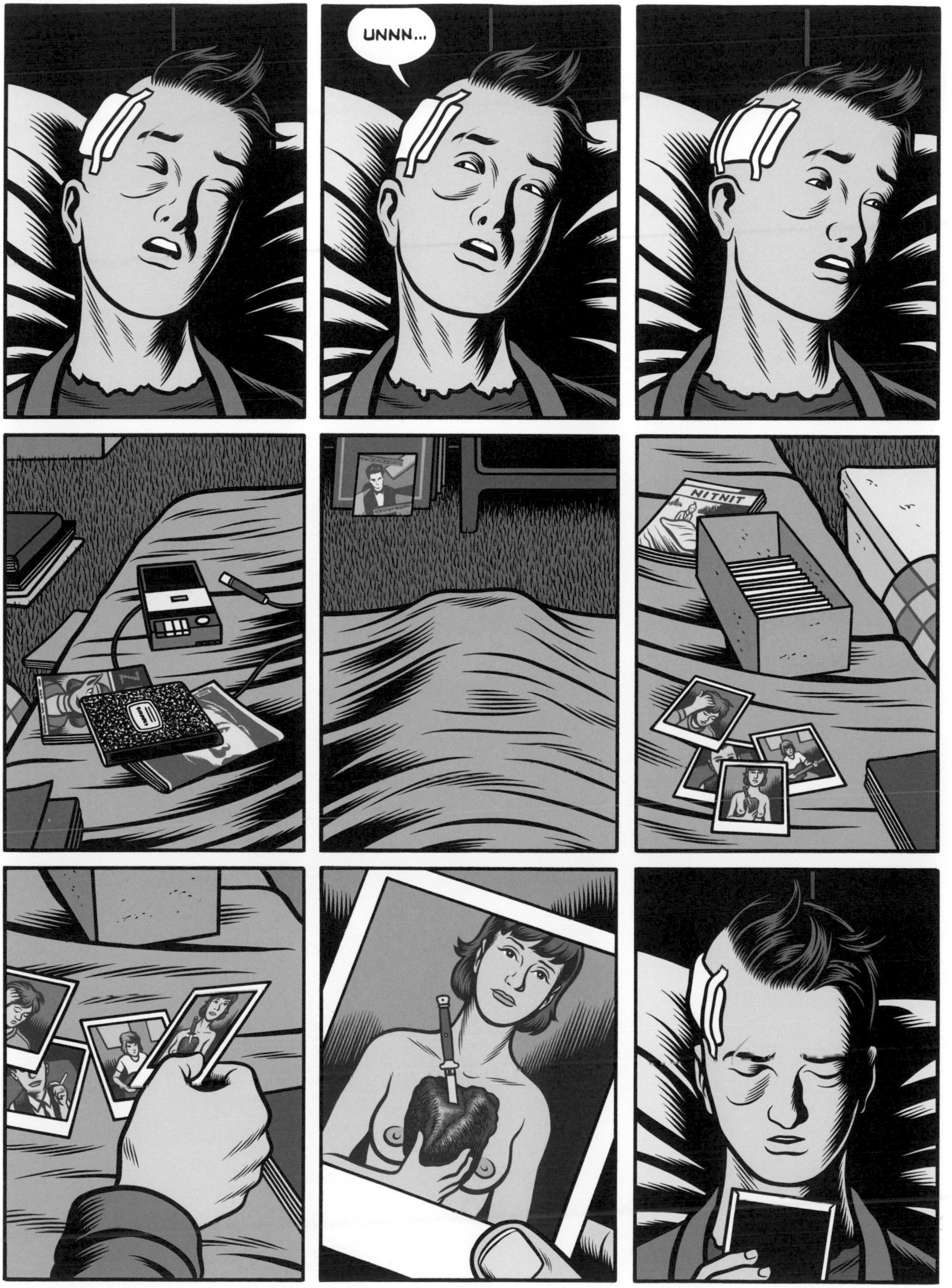
UNNN...
NITNIT

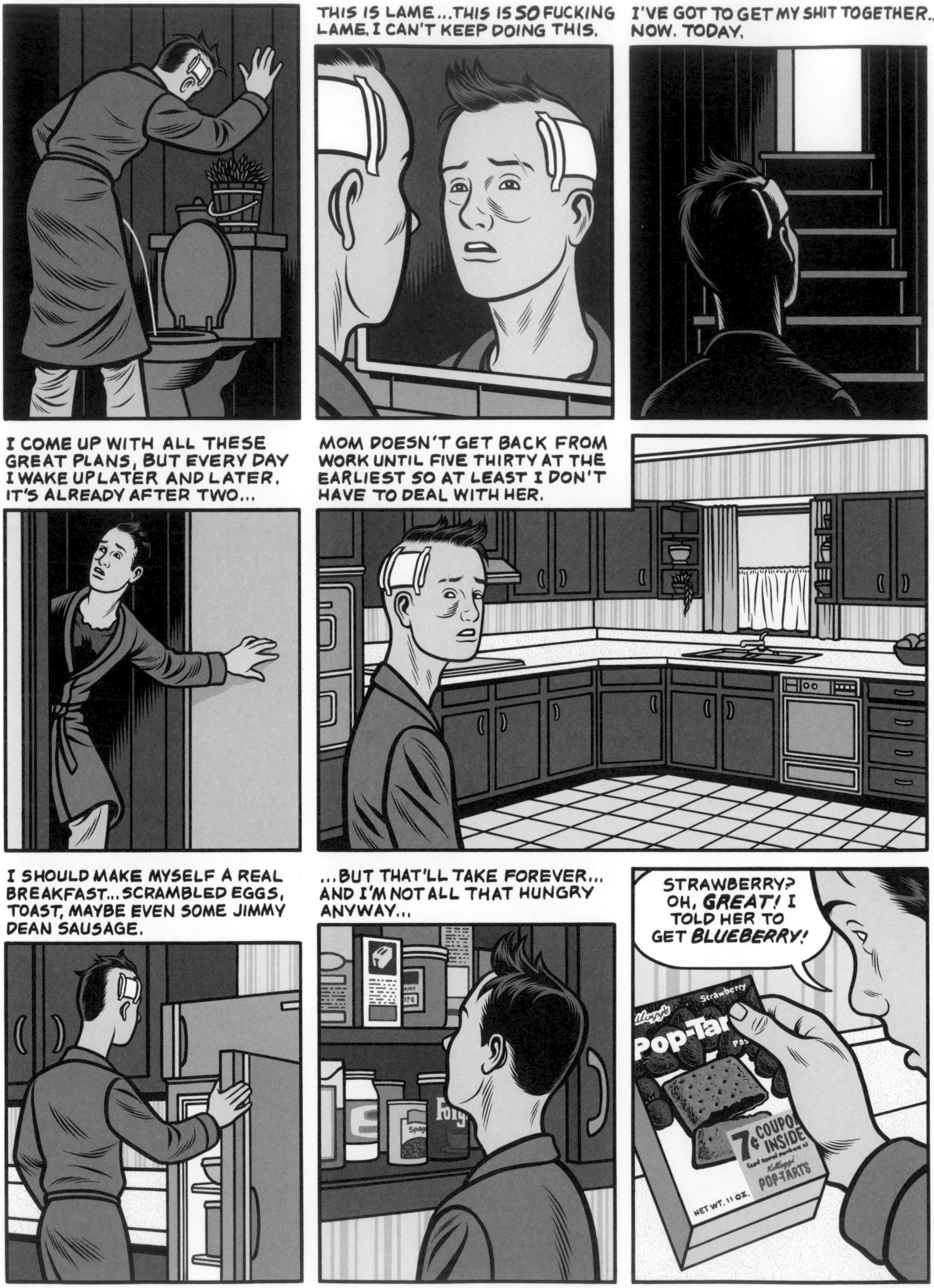
THIS IS LAME...THIS IS SO FUCKING LAME. I CAN'T KEEP DOING THIS.
I'VE GOT TO GET MY SHIT TOGETHER... NOW. TODAY.
I COME UP WITH ALL THESE GREAT PLANS, BUT EVERY DAY I WAKE UP LATER AND LATER. IT'S ALREADY AFTER TWO...
MOM DOESN'T GET BACK FROM WORK UNTIL FIVE THIRTY AT THE EARLIEST SO AT LEAST I DON'T HAVE TO DEAL WITH HER.
I SHOULD MAKE MYSELF A REAL BREAKFAST... SCRAMBLED EGGS, TOAST, MAYBE EVEN SOME JIMMY DEAN SAUSAGE.
...BUT THAT'LL TAKE FOREVER... AND I'M NOT ALL THAT HUNGRY ANYWAY...
STRAWBERRY? OH, GREAT! I TOLD HER TO GET BLUEBERRY!
Strawberry
NET WT. 11 OZ.

MMM...SMELLS SO GOOD. BUT I SHOULD WAIT A FEW SECONDS TO LET THEM COOL DOWN.

I DON'T WANT TO BURN MY TONGUE LIKE LAST TIME. I'VE GOTTA LEARN TO BE PATIENT.

...I'VE GOTTA

BZZZZZ!

AHHH! AW, SHIT!

COME ON, IT'S OKAY! IT'S ONLY THE DOORBELL! IT'S...IT'S THE MAILMAN OR...WHO THE FUCK KNOWS? BUT I DON'T HAVE TO ANSWER IT.

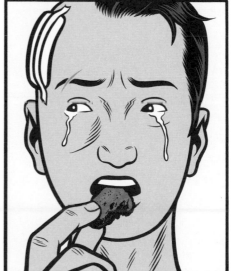

IF ANYONE ASKS, I CAN JUST SAY I WAS DOWNSTAIRS, SICK IN BED AND COULDN'T GET UP TO ANSWER THE DOOR...

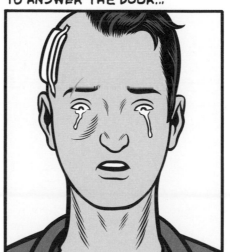

...AND IT'S TRUE. I FEEL AWFUL, I FEEL LIKE SHIT.

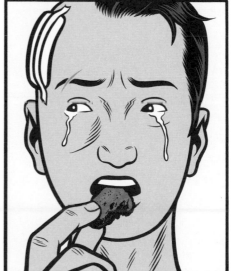

THIS ISN'T GOING TO LAST FOREVER.

IT CAN'T.

I'VE COUNTED OUT ALL OF MY PILLS AND IT'S ONLY A MATTER OF TIME...

IT'S GOING TO COME TO AN END NO MATTER WHAT...'CAUSE THERE'S ALWAYS A LAST *EVERYTHING*, RIGHT?

...YOUR LAST PILL, YOUR LAST CIGARETTE, YOUR LAST SIP OF WATER...

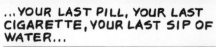

...YOUR LAST GOOD KISS.

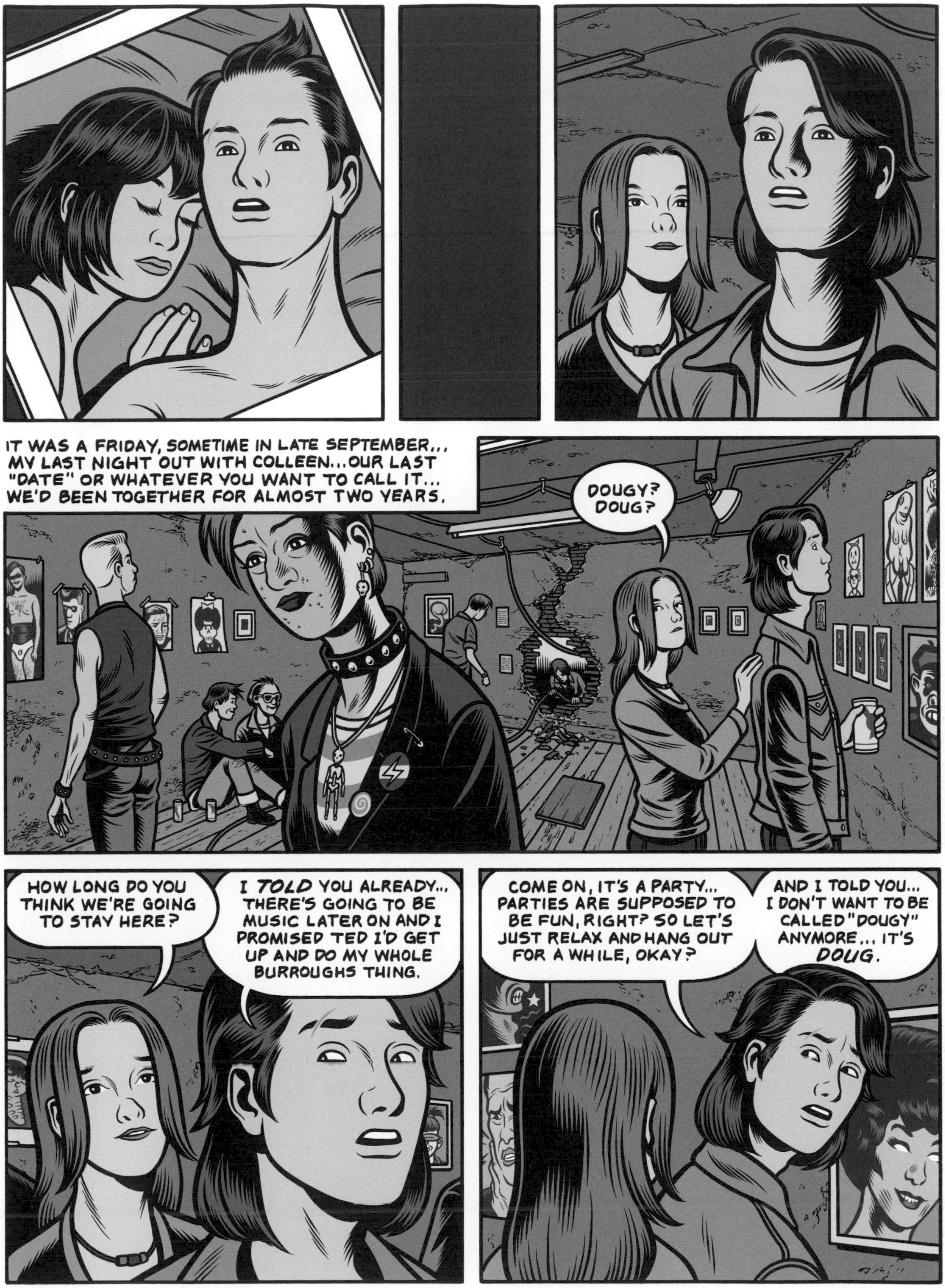
IT WAS A FRIDAY, SOMETIME IN LATE SEPTEMBER... MY LAST NIGHT OUT WITH COLLEEN... OUR LAST "DATE" OR WHATEVER YOU WANT TO CALL IT... WE'D BEEN TOGETHER FOR ALMOST TWO YEARS.
DOUGY? DOUG?
HOW LONG DO YOU THINK WE'RE GOING TO STAY HERE?
I *TOLD* YOU ALREADY... THERE'S GOING TO BE MUSIC LATER ON AND I PROMISED TED I'D GET UP AND DO MY WHOLE BURROUGHS THING.
COME ON, IT'S A PARTY... PARTIES ARE SUPPOSED TO BE FUN, RIGHT? SO LET'S JUST RELAX AND HANG OUT FOR A WHILE, OKAY?
AND I TOLD YOU... I DON'T WANT TO BE CALLED "DOUGY" ANYMORE... IT'S *DOUG*.

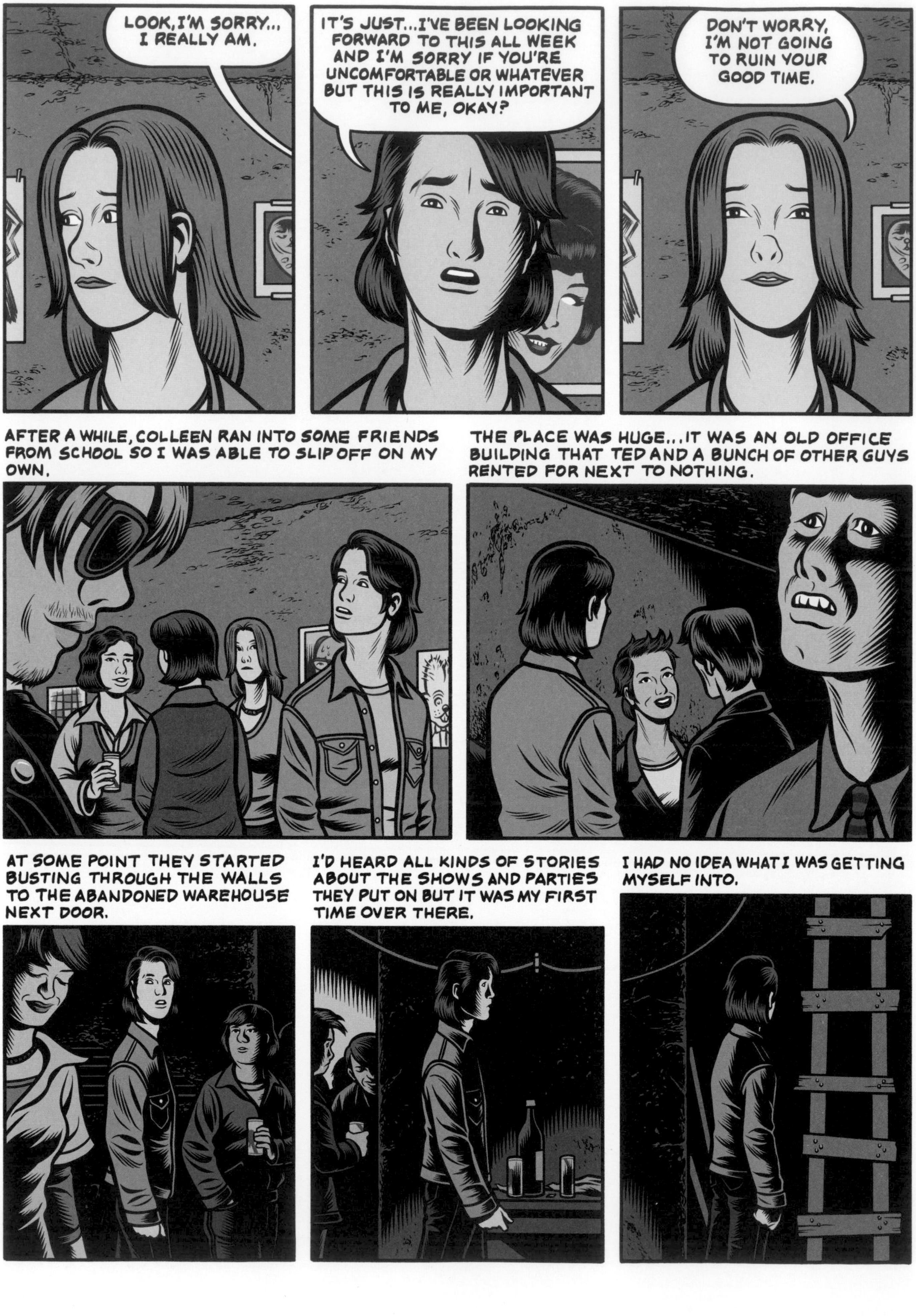
LOOK, I'M SORRY... I REALLY AM.
IT'S JUST...I'VE BEEN LOOKING FORWARD TO THIS ALL WEEK AND I'M SORRY IF YOU'RE UNCOMFORTABLE OR WHATEVER BUT THIS IS REALLY IMPORTANT TO ME, OKAY?
DON'T WORRY, I'M NOT GOING TO RUIN YOUR GOOD TIME.
AFTER A WHILE, COLLEEN RAN INTO SOME FRIENDS FROM SCHOOL SO I WAS ABLE TO SLIP OFF ON MY OWN.
THE PLACE WAS HUGE...IT WAS AN OLD OFFICE BUILDING THAT TED AND A BUNCH OF OTHER GUYS RENTED FOR NEXT TO NOTHING.
AT SOME POINT THEY STARTED BUSTING THROUGH THE WALLS TO THE ABANDONED WAREHOUSE NEXT DOOR.
I'D HEARD ALL KINDS OF STORIES ABOUT THE SHOWS AND PARTIES THEY PUT ON BUT IT WAS MY FIRST TIME OVER THERE.
I HAD NO IDEA WHAT I WAS GETTING MYSELF INTO.

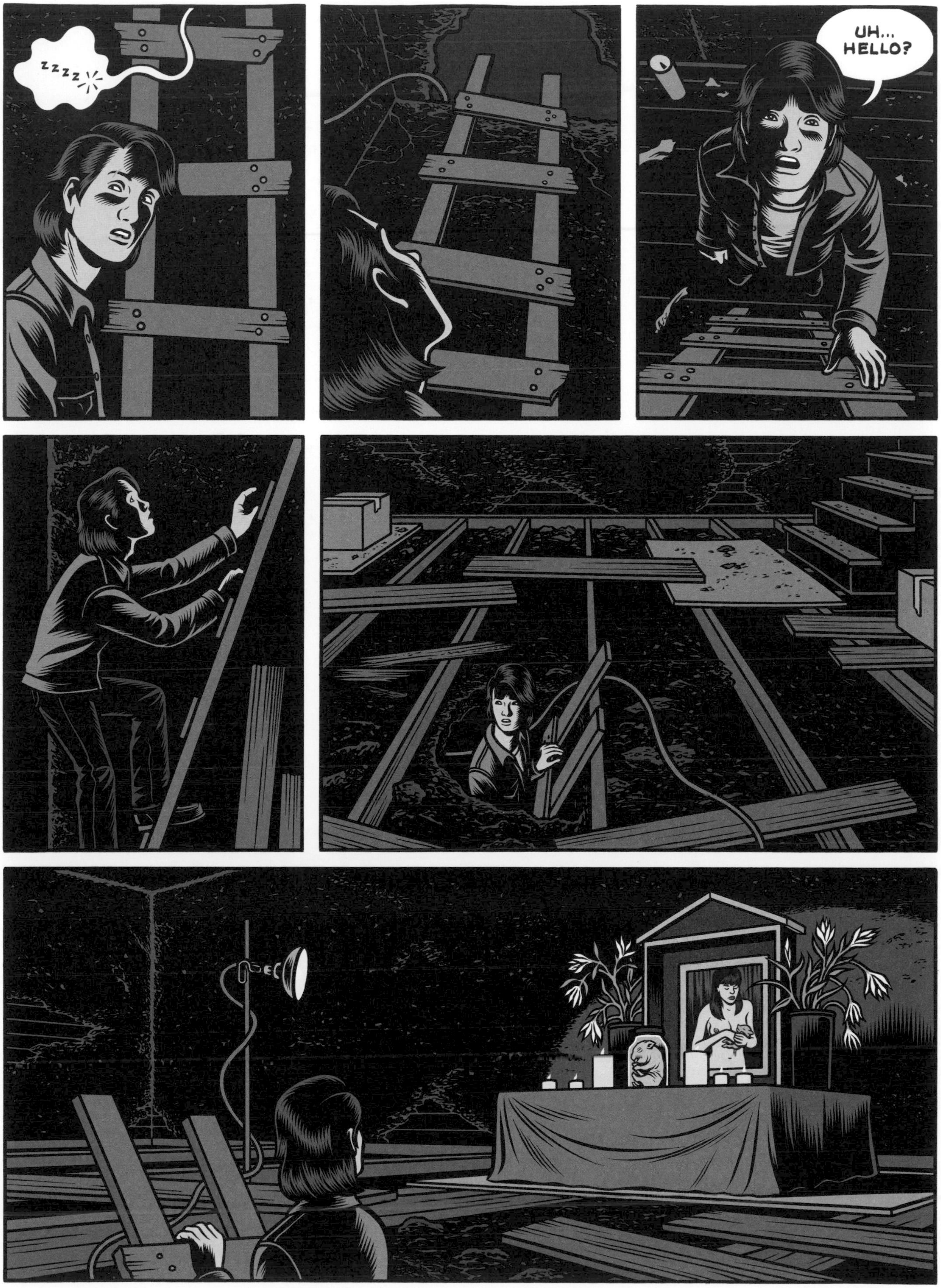
ZZZZ
UH... HELLO?

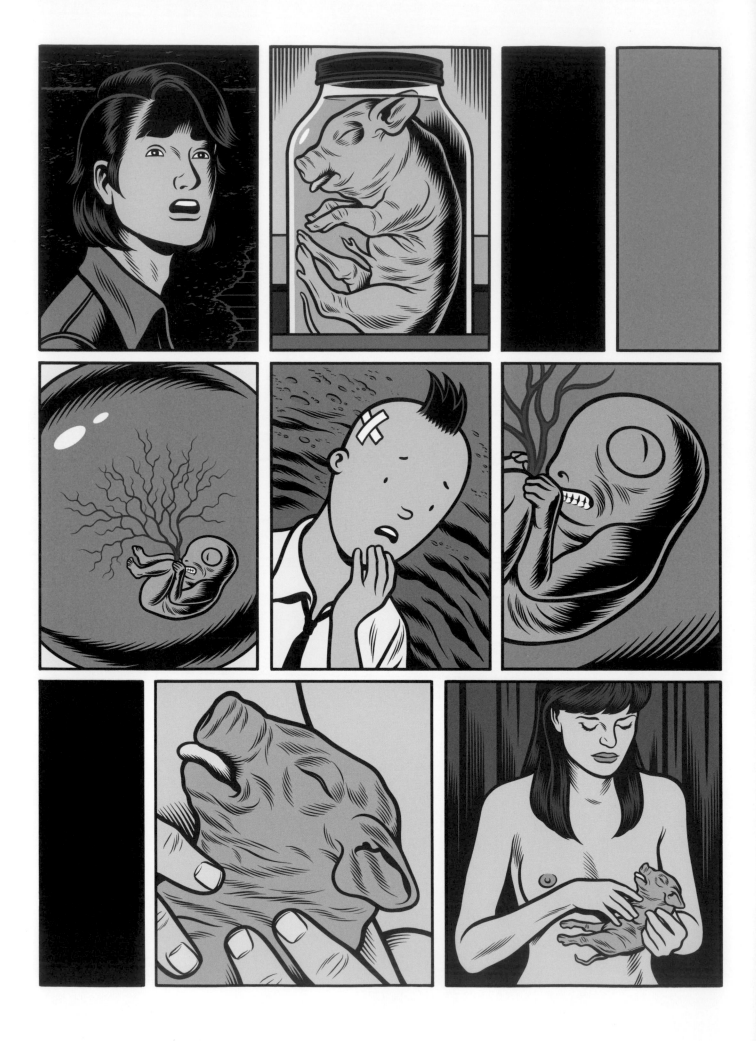

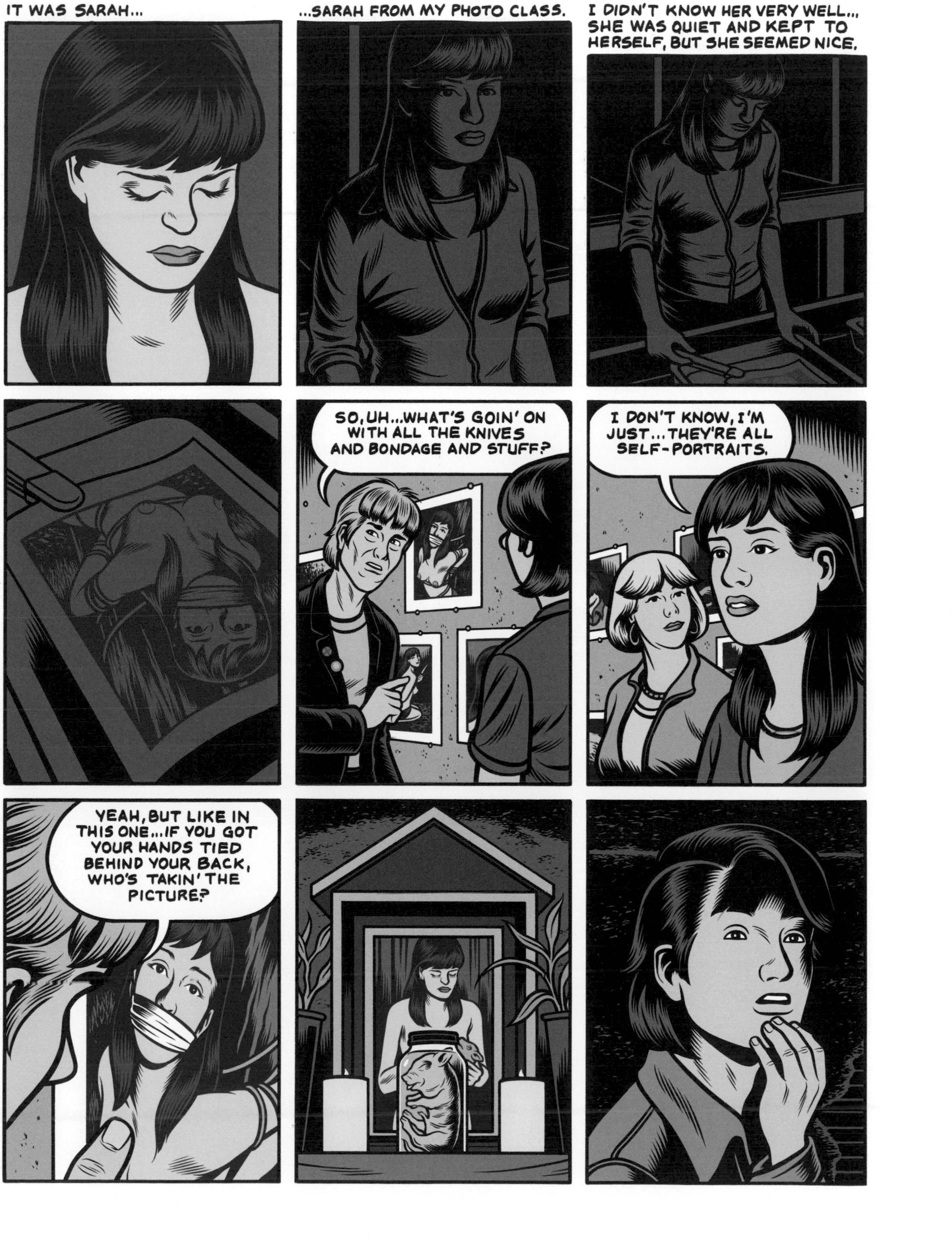
IT WAS SARAH...
...SARAH FROM MY PHOTO CLASS.
I DIDN'T KNOW HER VERY WELL... SHE WAS QUIET AND KEPT TO HERSELF, BUT SHE SEEMED NICE.
SO, UH...WHAT'S GOIN' ON WITH ALL THE KNIVES AND BONDAGE AND STUFF?
I DON'T KNOW, I'M JUST...THEY'RE ALL SELF-PORTRAITS.
YEAH, BUT LIKE IN THIS ONE...IF YOU GOT YOUR HANDS TIED BEHIND YOUR BACK, WHO'S TAKIN' THE PICTURE?

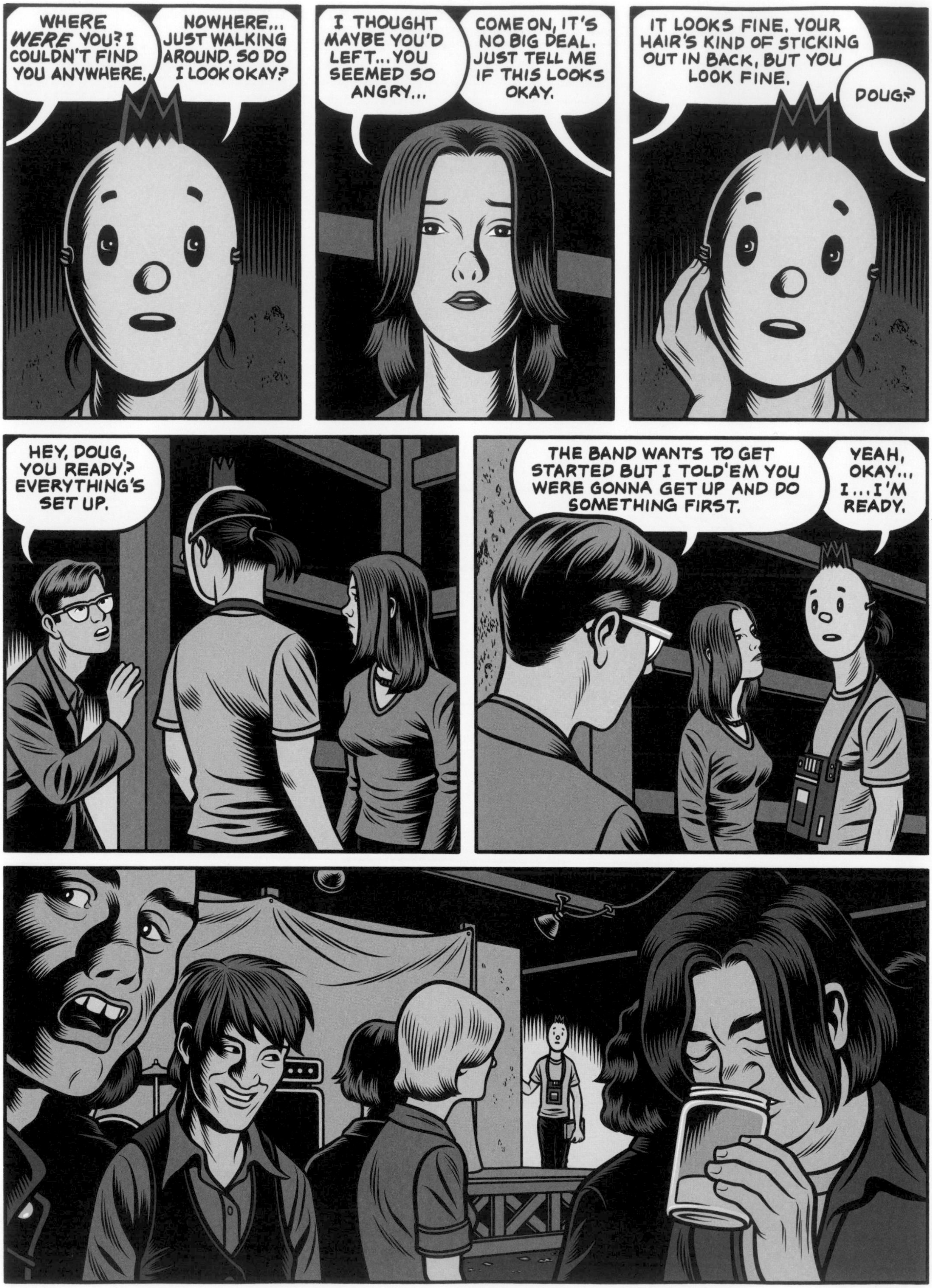
WHERE *WERE* YOU? I COULDN'T FIND YOU ANYWHERE.
NOWHERE... JUST WALKING AROUND. SO DO I LOOK OKAY?
I THOUGHT MAYBE YOU'D LEFT... YOU SEEMED SO ANGRY...
COME ON, IT'S NO BIG DEAL. JUST TELL ME IF THIS LOOKS OKAY.
IT LOOKS FINE. YOUR HAIR'S KIND OF STICKING OUT IN BACK, BUT YOU LOOK FINE.
DOUG?
HEY, DOUG, YOU READY? EVERYTHING'S SET UP.
THE BAND WANTS TO GET STARTED BUT I TOLD'EM YOU WERE GONNA GET UP AND DO SOMETHING FIRST.
YEAH, OKAY..., I...I'M READY.

I WAS SCARED SHITLESS. I'D DONE A COUPLE OF PERFORMANCES BEFORE BUT NEVER IN FRONT OF A REAL AUDIENCE.

HI, I'M NITNIT, ALSO KNOWN AS JOHNNY 23.

I HAD A TAPE I'D MADE OF RANDOM SOUNDS...GUITAR FEEDBACK, TELEVISION COMMERCIALS, WHITE NOISE...

DON'T WORRY, THIS WON'T TAKE LONG.

KLIK☀SSHHHH

THE IDEA WAS TO BLAST THE TAPE AS LOUD AS POSSIBLE AND THEN READ A FEW OF MY CUT-UPS ON TOP OF THAT.

ZZZZZZ ZZZZZZZZ ZZZ

THIS IS THE ONLY PART WHERE I WAKE A DISTANT FLICKER ABOUT THE FLOOD

TTTTTT FFFFFFFFHHHHHHHHHAAAA

SWOLLEN RIVER JUST A GHOST IN A VAST MUTTERING COLORS BLOOMING...

VVVVVVMMMMAAAAAAAANNNNNZZZZ

THIN PINK BLANKET OLD PHOTOS FADING IN FLOATING DOWN THE ROTTEN DAWN WIND

VVVVVVVVMMAAK☀AKK☀ AKK!

FEELING EGG FLESH CRUEL IDIOT SMILES GREEN BOYS WITH DO I WANT TO LOOK...

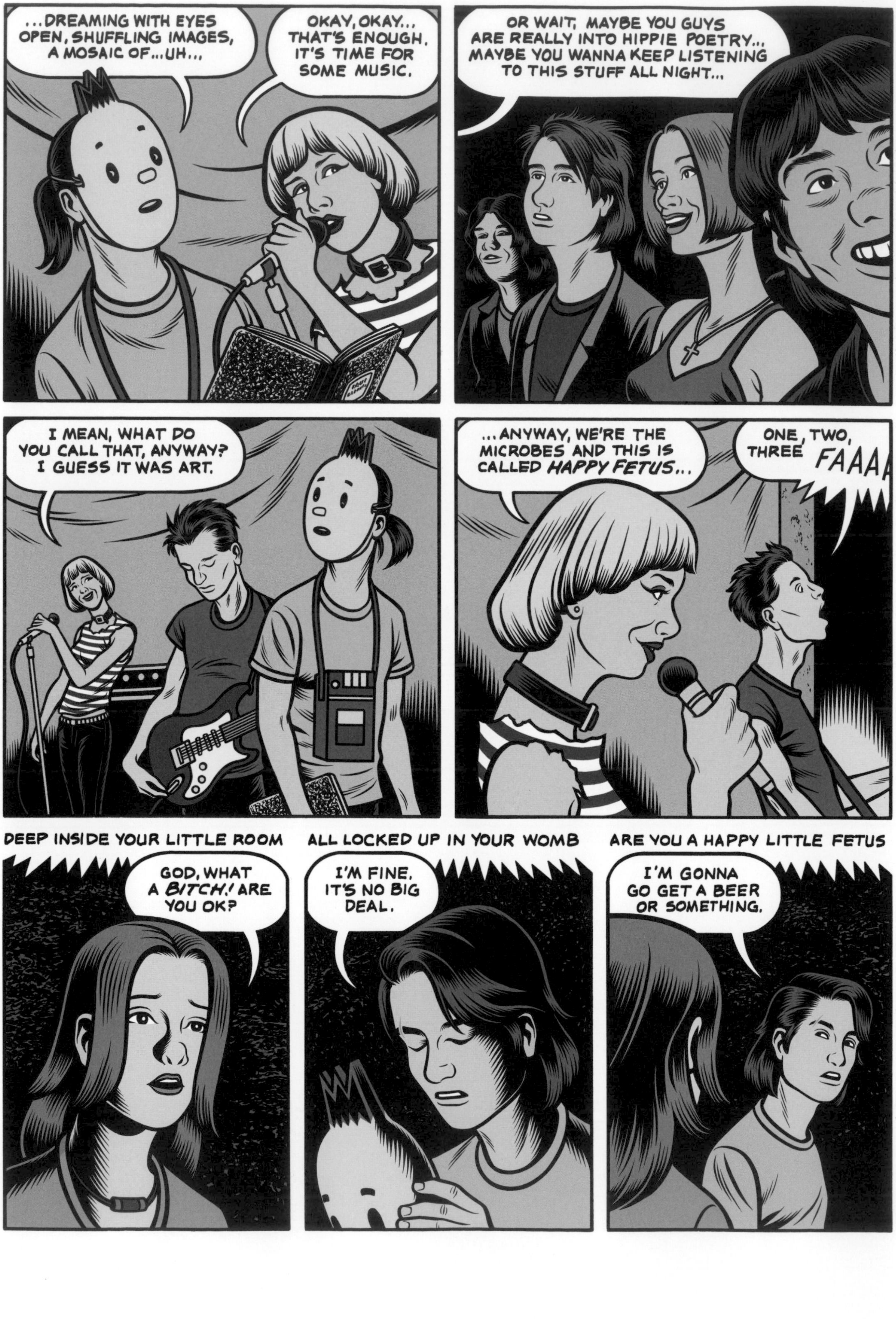
...DREAMING WITH EYES OPEN, SHUFFLING IMAGES, A MOSAIC OF...UH...
OKAY, OKAY... THAT'S ENOUGH. IT'S TIME FOR SOME MUSIC.
OR WAIT, MAYBE YOU GUYS ARE REALLY INTO HIPPIE POETRY... MAYBE YOU WANNA KEEP LISTENING TO THIS STUFF ALL NIGHT...
I MEAN, WHAT DO YOU CALL THAT, ANYWAY? I GUESS IT WAS ART.
...ANYWAY, WE'RE THE MICROBES AND THIS IS CALLED *HAPPY FETUS*...
ONE, TWO, THREE
FAAAA
DEEP INSIDE YOUR LITTLE ROOM
GOD, WHAT A *BITCH!* ARE YOU OK?
ALL LOCKED UP IN YOUR WOMB
I'M FINE. IT'S NO BIG DEAL.
ARE YOU A HAPPY LITTLE FETUS
I'M GONNA GO GET A BEER OR SOMETHING.

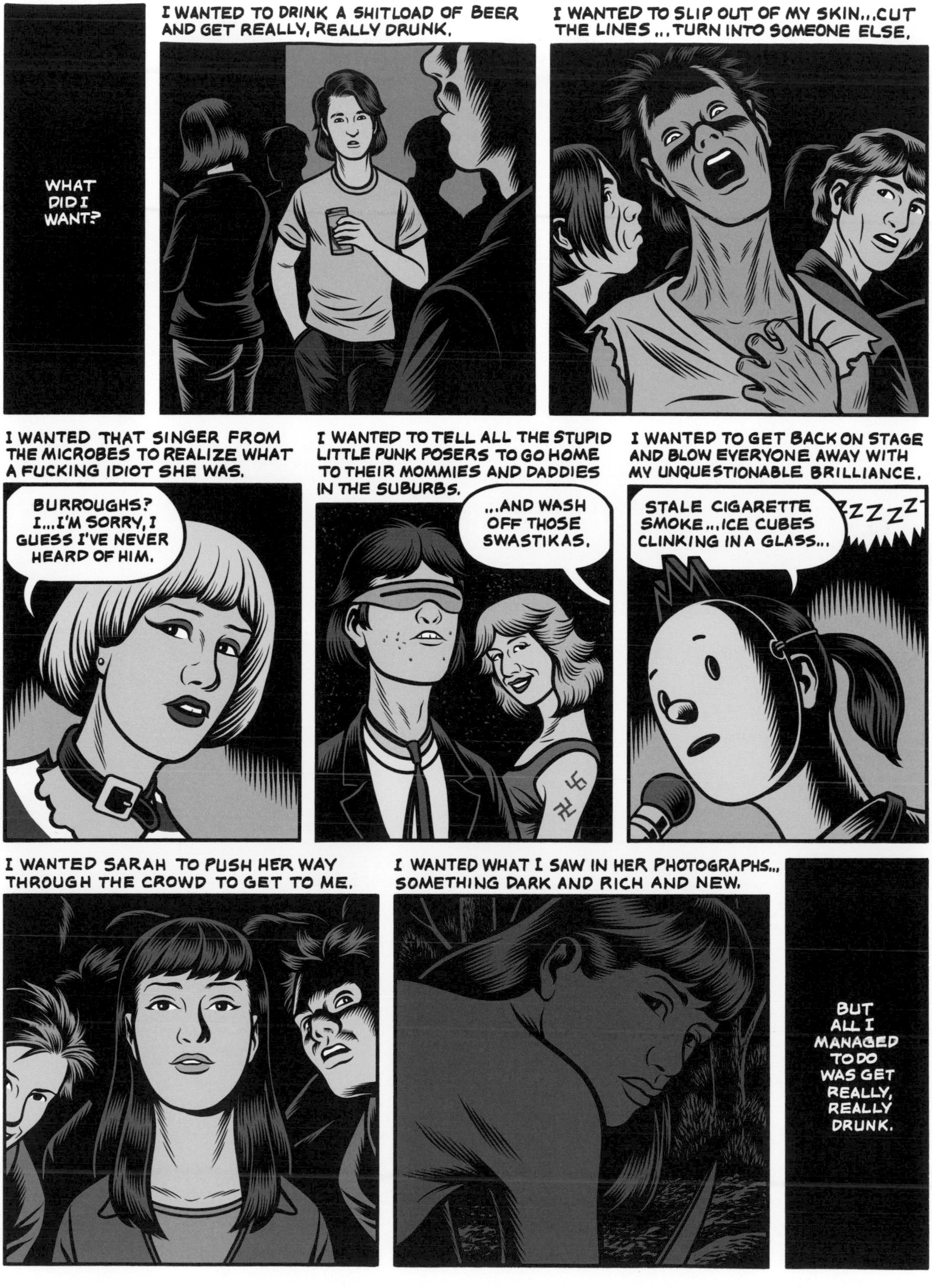
WHAT DID I WANT?
I WANTED TO DRINK A SHITLOAD OF BEER AND GET REALLY, REALLY DRUNK.
I WANTED TO SLIP OUT OF MY SKIN...CUT THE LINES ... TURN INTO SOMEONE ELSE.
I WANTED THAT SINGER FROM THE MICROBES TO REALIZE WHAT A FUCKING IDIOT SHE WAS.
BURROUGHS? I...I'M SORRY, I GUESS I'VE NEVER HEARD OF HIM.
I WANTED TO TELL ALL THE STUPID LITTLE PUNK POSERS TO GO HOME TO THEIR MOMMIES AND DADDIES IN THE SUBURBS.
...AND WASH OFF THOSE SWASTIKAS.
I WANTED TO GET BACK ON STAGE AND BLOW EVERYONE AWAY WITH MY UNQUESTIONABLE BRILLIANCE.
STALE CIGARETTE SMOKE...ICE CUBES CLINKING IN A GLASS...
ZZZZZ
I WANTED SARAH TO PUSH HER WAY THROUGH THE CROWD TO GET TO ME.
I WANTED WHAT I SAW IN HER PHOTOGRAPHS... SOMETHING DARK AND RICH AND NEW.
BUT ALL I MANAGED TO DO WAS GET REALLY, REALLY DRUNK.

WE HAVE TO GO... I MEAN IT. I CAN'T TAKE ANY MORE OF THIS.

YOU JUST DON'T UNDERSTAND... GOD...IF... IF YOU COULD JUST... IF YOU COULD LOOK INSIDE MY HEAD, YOU'D KNOW.

WHAT'RE YOU TALKING ABOUT?

FUCK IT...I GIVE UP. LET ME GET MY STUFF AND WE'LL GO.

WE ALMOST MADE IT OUT OF THERE...IF WE'D LEFT A FEW MINUTES EARLIER THERE'S A GOOD CHANCE NONE OF THIS SHIT WOULD HAVE HAPPENED.

WATCH OUT, THERE'S SOME BROKEN GLASS OVER HERE.

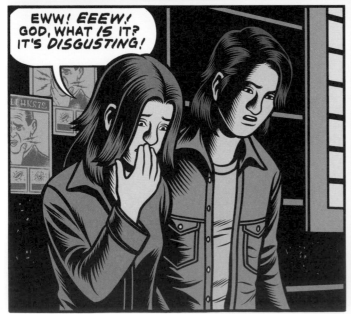

EWW! EEEW! GOD, WHAT IS IT? IT'S DISGUSTING!

NO, IT'S... UH... IT'S SARAH'S.

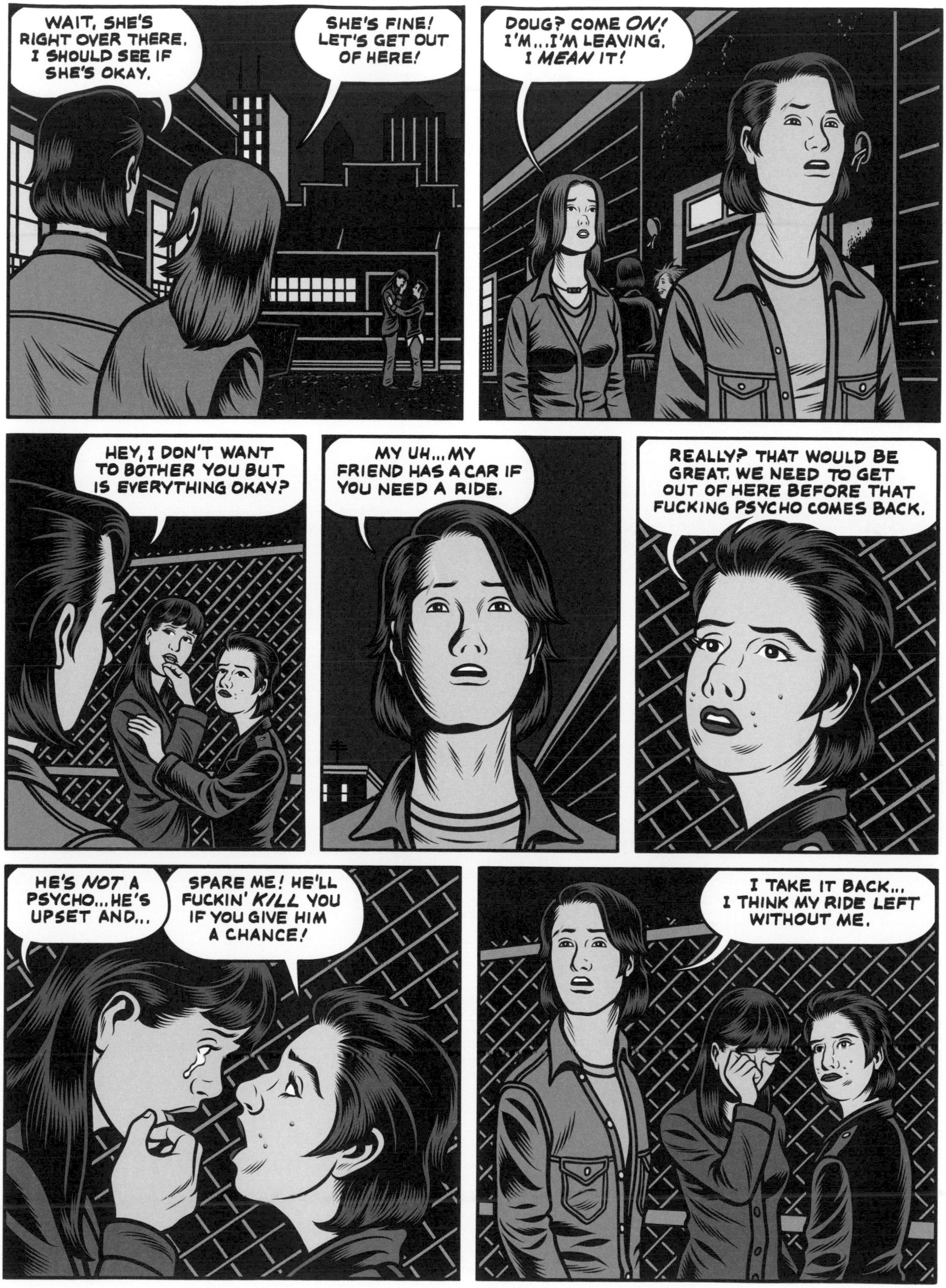
WAIT, SHE'S RIGHT OVER THERE. I SHOULD SEE IF SHE'S OKAY.
SHE'S FINE! LET'S GET OUT OF HERE!
DOUG? COME *ON*! I'M...I'M LEAVING. I *MEAN* IT!
HEY, I DON'T WANT TO BOTHER YOU BUT IS EVERYTHING OKAY?
MY UH... MY FRIEND HAS A CAR IF YOU NEED A RIDE.
REALLY? THAT WOULD BE GREAT. WE NEED TO GET OUT OF HERE BEFORE THAT FUCKING PSYCHO COMES BACK.
HE'S *NOT* A PSYCHO... HE'S UPSET AND...
SPARE ME! HE'LL FUCKIN' *KILL* YOU IF YOU GIVE HIM A CHANCE!
I TAKE IT BACK... I THINK MY RIDE LEFT WITHOUT ME.

SHE WAS DRIVING AWAY SLOWLY... GIVING ME ONE LAST CHANCE. I COULD HAVE CHASED AFTER HER AND APOLOGIZED...

...BUT WHAT DID I DO? I TURNED AWAY... TURNED MY BACK ON HER WITHOUT THINKING TWICE.

I'VE GOT TO TAPER OFF SLOWLY... I REALLY DO. OTHERWISE I'M GONNA BE SICK AS A DOG.

I'VE COUNTED OUT ALL MY PILLS... I'VE EVEN DRAWN UP A LITTLE CALENDAR ... A SCHEDULE.

BUT THOSE LAST FOUR PILLS HARDLY DID ANYTHING... AND I NEED TO GET WARM.

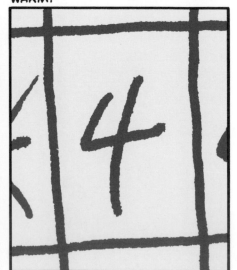

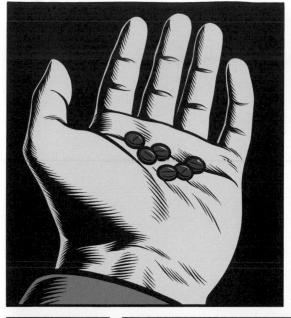

THERE'S NEVER ENOUGH.

EVEN WHEN I FINALLY MANAGE TO KNOCK MYSELF OUT... WHEN I'M DEAD ASLEEP...

EVEN THEN THE IMAGES SLIP IN...

...SEEP DOWN INTO THE BACK OF MY HEAD AND COME UP BEHIND MY EYES.

THE SAME STUFF OVER AND OVER AGAIN...

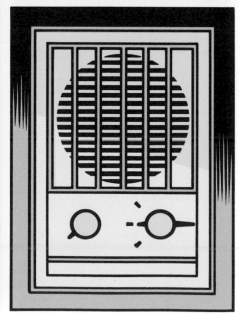

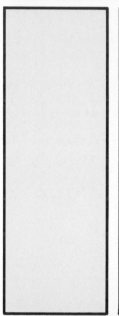

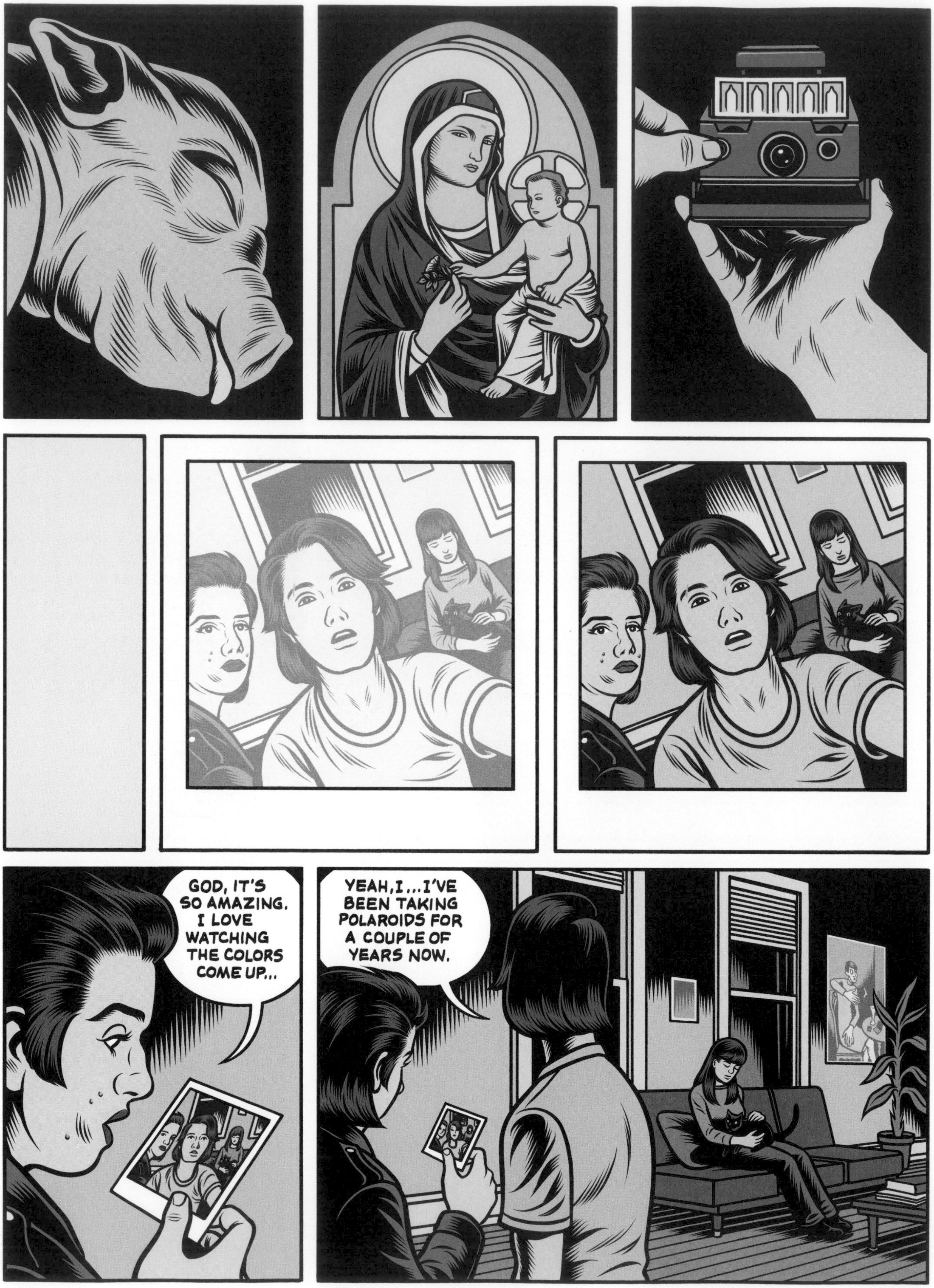
GOD, IT'S SO AMAZING. I LOVE WATCHING THE COLORS COME UP...
YEAH, I...I'VE BEEN TAKING POLAROIDS FOR A COUPLE OF YEARS NOW.

I'M WORKING ON THIS SERIES OF SELF-PORTRAITS WHERE I...
HEY, WE NEED SOME BEER! YOU GUYS UP FOR BEER?
HERE YOU GO...NICE PICTURE.
I'M PRETTY SURE WE STILL GOT A QUART OF MILLER...I'LL GO WASH SOME GLASSES.
SO...UH...HAVE YOU EVER HEARD OF THIS ARTIST CALLED LUCAS SAMARAS? HE TAKES POLAROIDS TOO.
HE DOES THESE SELF-PORTRAITS WHERE HE SETS UP A WHOLE ENVIRONMENT IN HIS APARTMENT WITH COLORED LIGHTS AND ALL KINDS OF WEIRD STUFF...
...AND HE DOES THIS THING WHERE HE MANIPULATES THE EMULSION OF THE FILM...PUSHES IT AROUND AND...AND I THINK YOU'D REALLY LIKE THEM.
BZZZZZZZ!

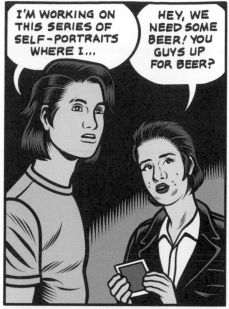

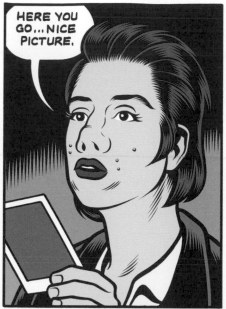

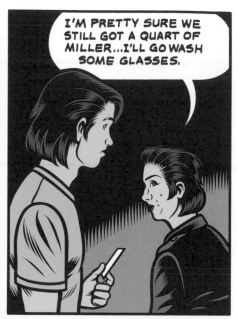

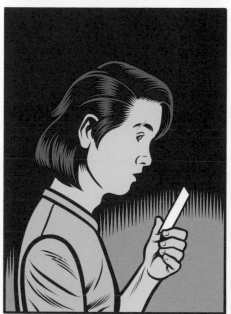

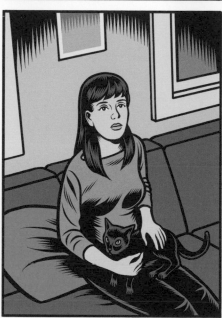

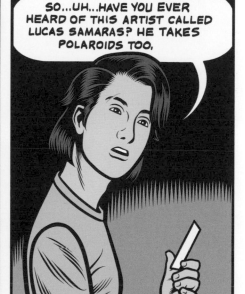

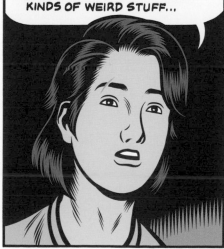

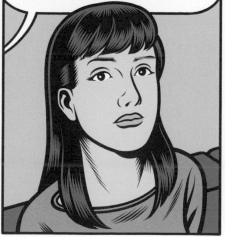

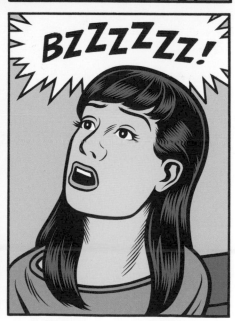

WAIT! LET ME GET IT! THAT'S HIM! THAT'S GOTTA BE HIM! DON'T SAY A WORD!
YEAH? WHO'S THERE?
NICKY? IT'S ME. I GOTTA TALK TO SARAH.
WELL, YOU KNOW WHAT? I DON'T THINK THAT'S GONNA HAPPEN. YOU WERE BEING A REAL ASSHOLE TONIGHT!
LOOK, I KNOW... I REALLY SCREWED UP, BUT I HAVE TO TALK TO HER...JUST OPEN THE DOOR.
I CAN'T DO THAT. SHE'S REALLY UPSET AND...AND SHE WENT TO BED, OKAY?
SHE'S IN BED?
WHO'S SHE WITH? SHE'S UP THERE WITH SOME GUY, ISN'T SHE?
WHO'S SHE FUCKING?

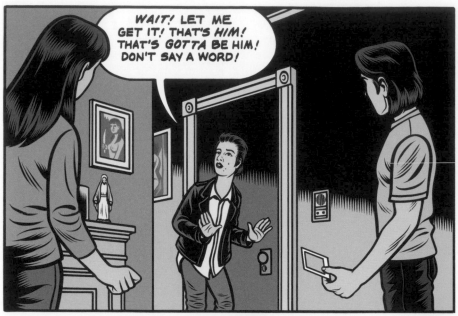

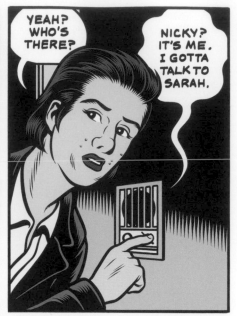

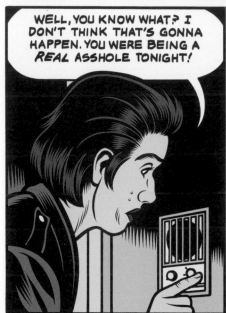

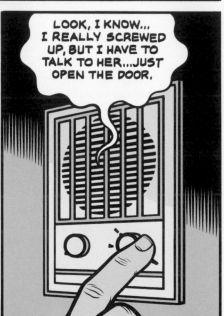

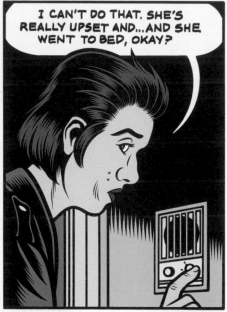

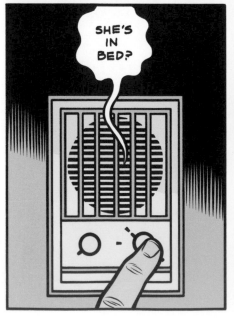

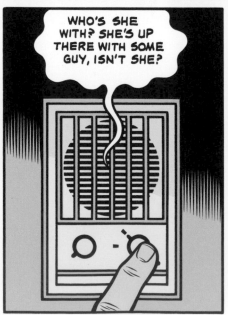

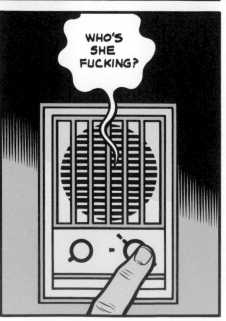

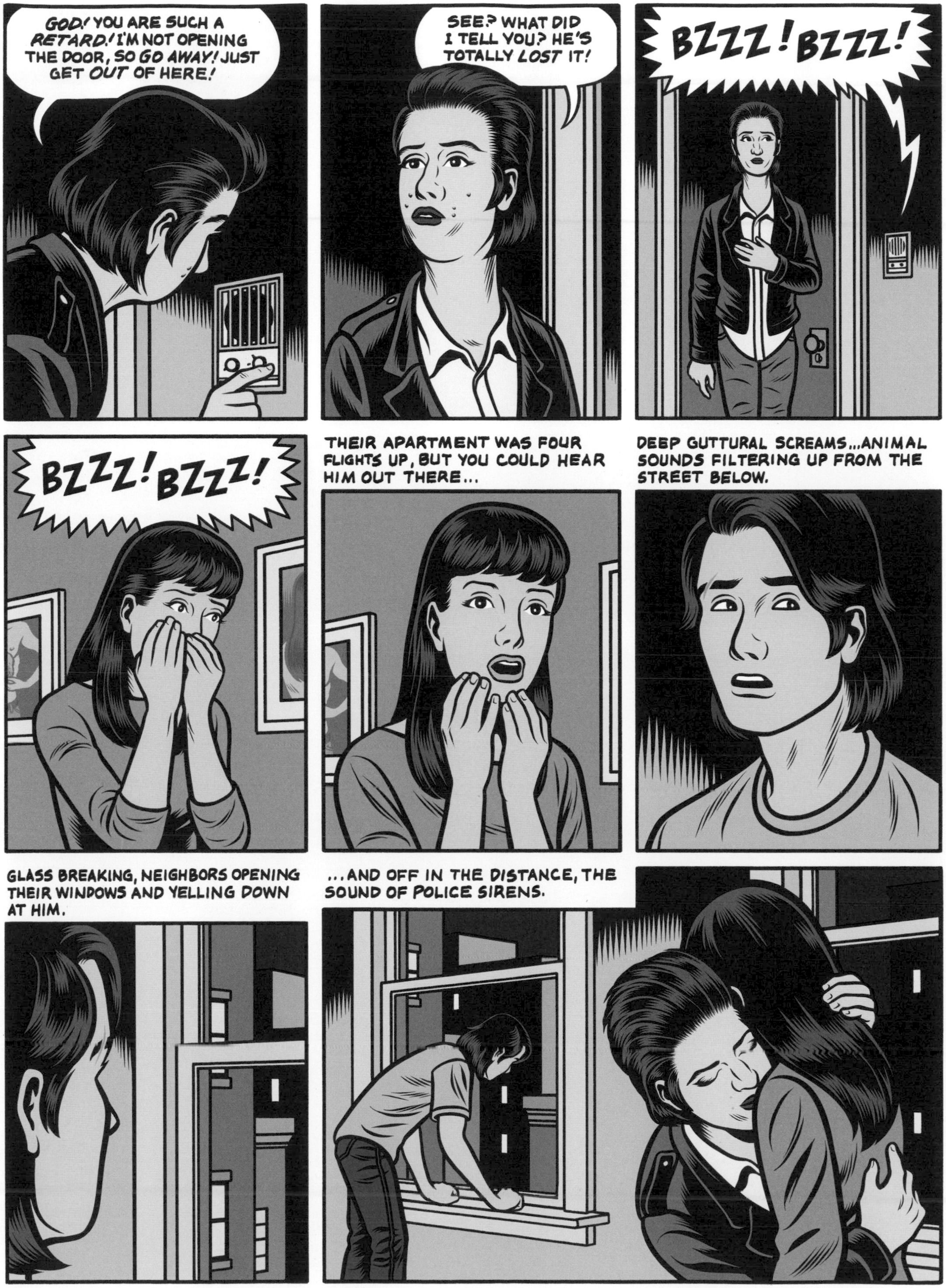
GOD! YOU ARE SUCH A RETARD! I'M NOT OPENING THE DOOR, SO GO AWAY! JUST GET OUT OF HERE!
SEE? WHAT DID I TELL YOU? HE'S TOTALLY LOST IT!
BZZZ! BZZZ!
BZZZ! BZZZ!
THEIR APARTMENT WAS FOUR FLIGHTS UP, BUT YOU COULD HEAR HIM OUT THERE...
DEEP GUTTURAL SCREAMS...ANIMAL SOUNDS FILTERING UP FROM THE STREET BELOW.
GLASS BREAKING, NEIGHBORS OPENING THEIR WINDOWS AND YELLING DOWN AT HIM.
...AND OFF IN THE DISTANCE, THE SOUND OF POLICE SIRENS.

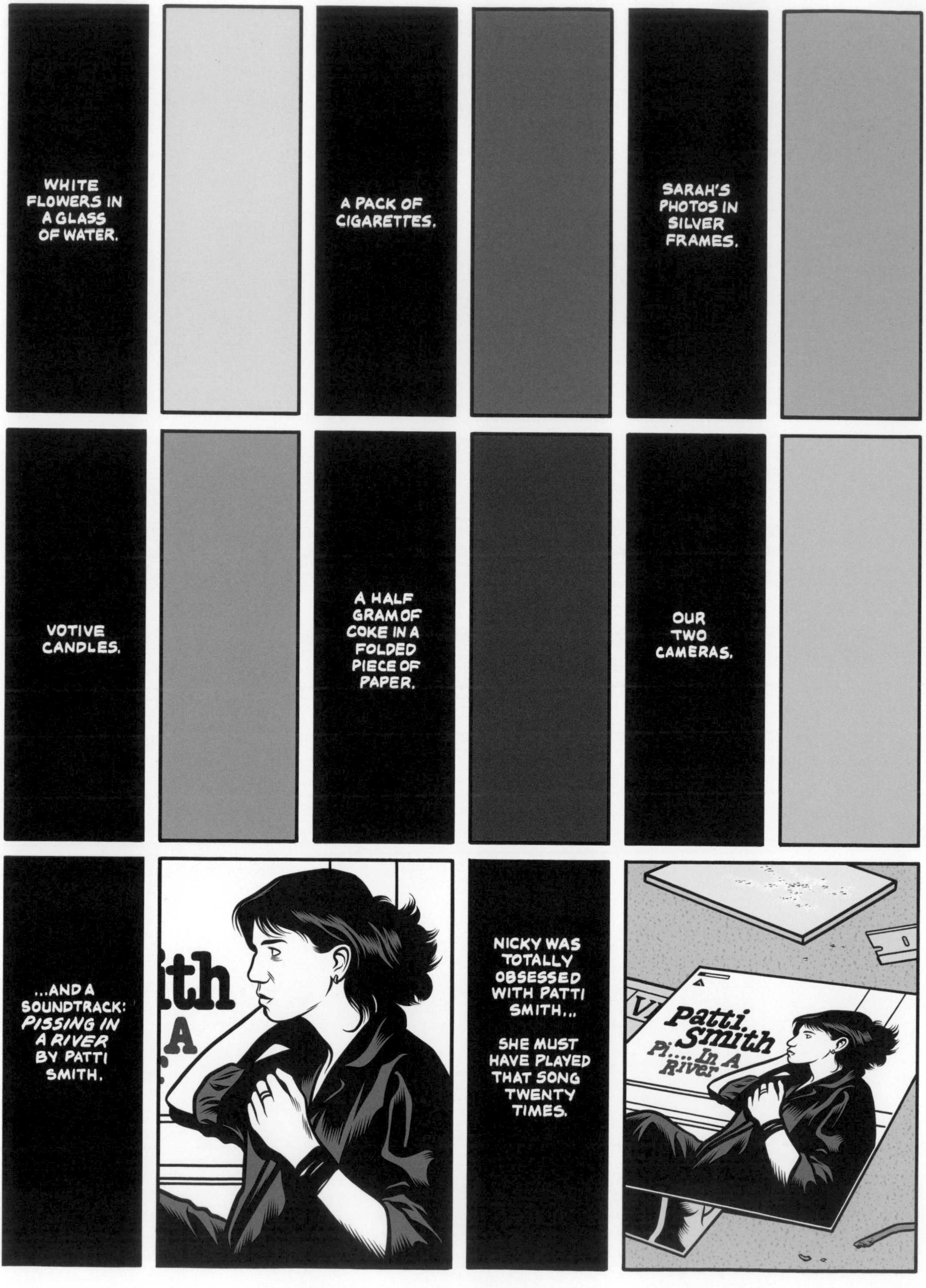
WHITE FLOWERS IN A GLASS OF WATER.
A PACK OF CIGARETTES.
SARAH'S PHOTOS IN SILVER FRAMES.
VOTIVE CANDLES.
A HALF GRAM OF COKE IN A FOLDED PIECE OF PAPER.
OUR TWO CAMERAS.
...AND A SOUNDTRACK: *PISSING IN A RIVER* BY PATTI SMITH.
NICKY WAS TOTALLY OBSESSED WITH PATTI SMITH...
SHE MUST HAVE PLAYED THAT SONG TWENTY TIMES.
Patti Smith
Pi.... In A River

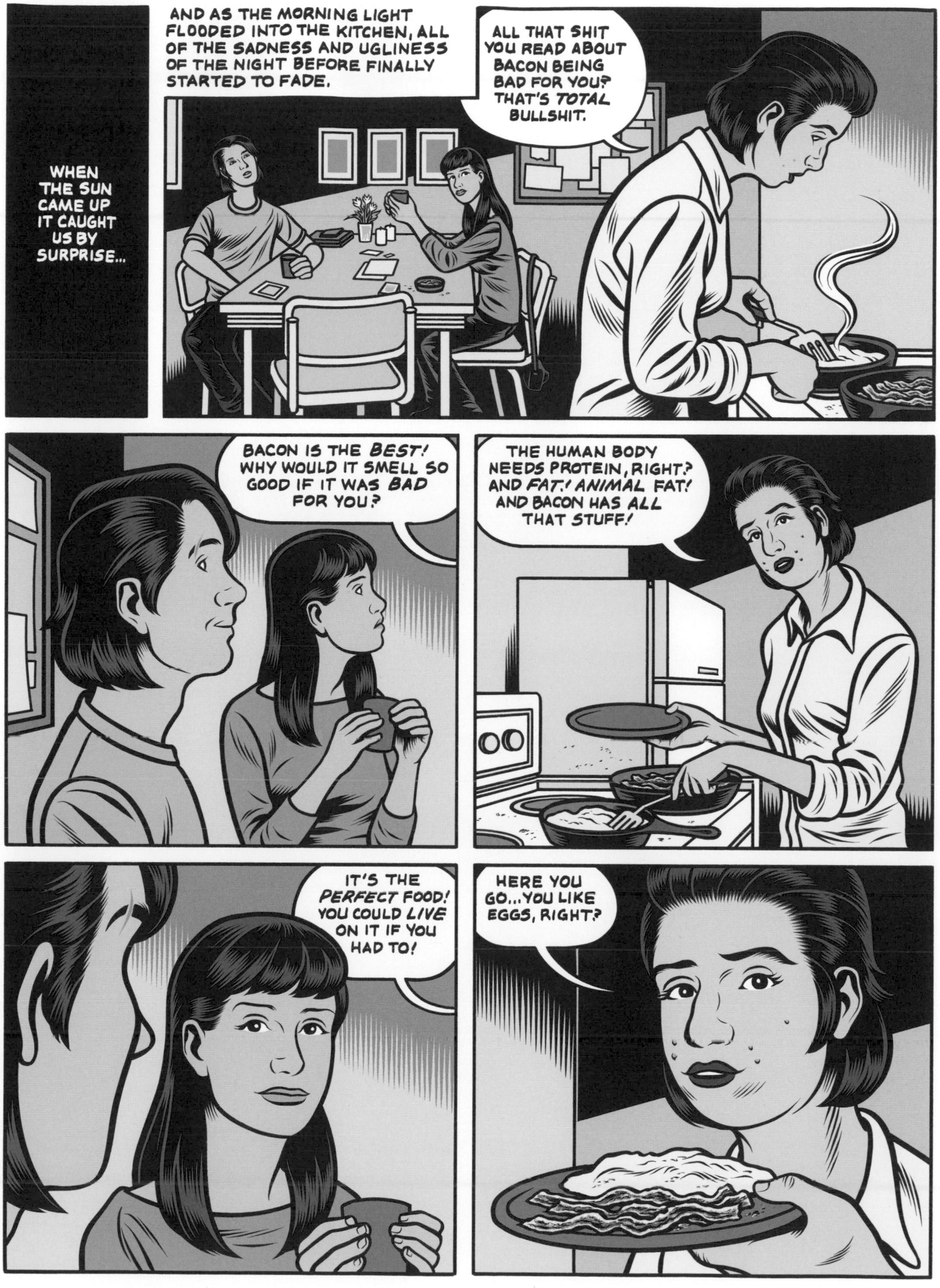
AND AS THE MORNING LIGHT FLOODED INTO THE KITCHEN, ALL OF THE SADNESS AND UGLINESS OF THE NIGHT BEFORE FINALLY STARTED TO FADE.
WHEN THE SUN CAME UP IT CAUGHT US BY SURPRISE...
ALL THAT SHIT YOU READ ABOUT BACON BEING BAD FOR YOU? THAT'S TOTAL BULLSHIT.
BACON IS THE BEST! WHY WOULD IT SMELL SO GOOD IF IT WAS BAD FOR YOU?
THE HUMAN BODY NEEDS PROTEIN, RIGHT? AND FAT! ANIMAL FAT! AND BACON HAS ALL THAT STUFF!
IT'S THE PERFECT FOOD! YOU COULD LIVE ON IT IF YOU HAD TO!
HERE YOU GO... YOU LIKE EGGS, RIGHT?

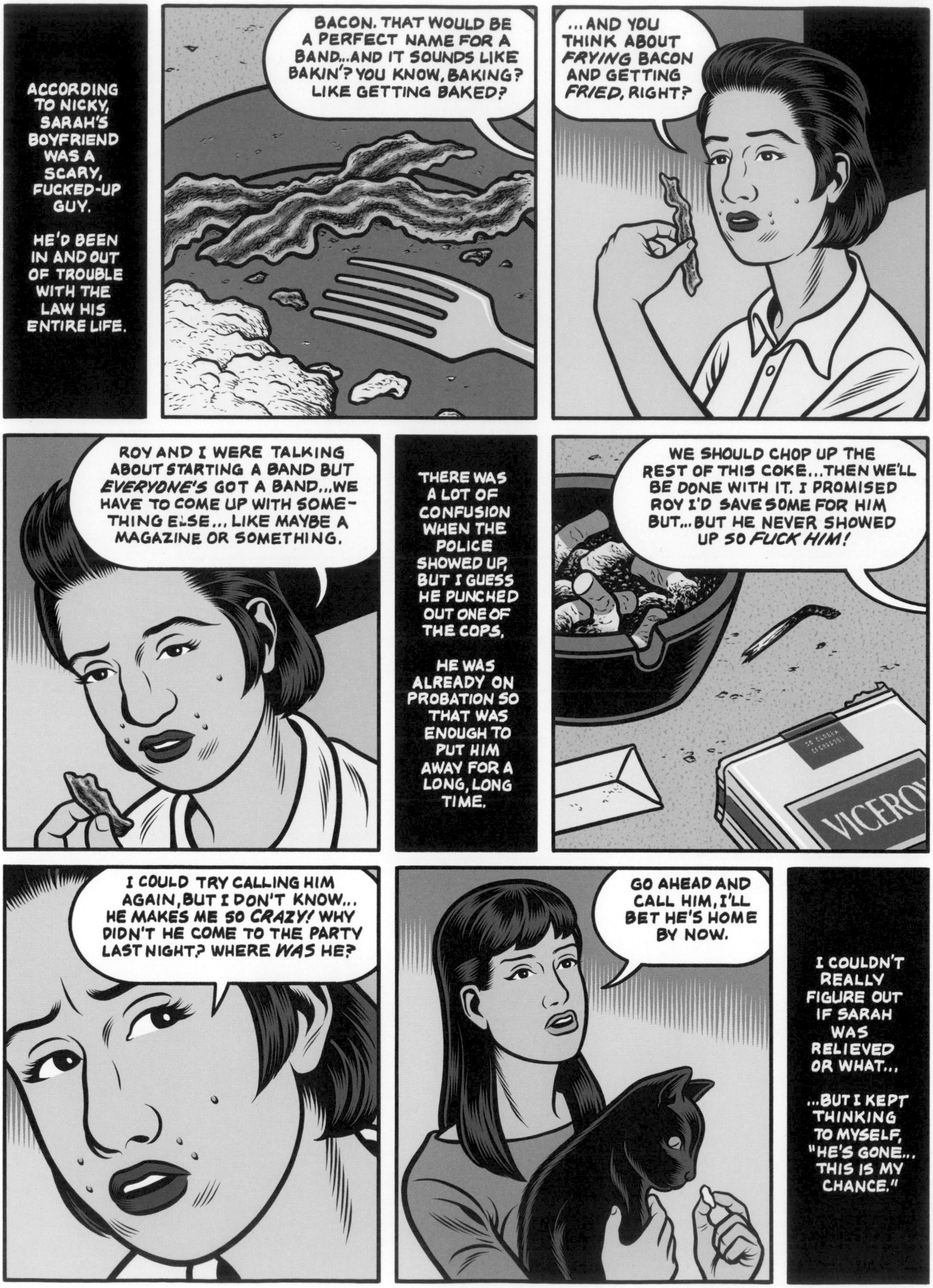

ACCORDING TO NICKY, SARAH'S BOYFRIEND WAS A SCARY, FUCKED-UP GUY.
HE'D BEEN IN AND OUT OF TROUBLE WITH THE LAW HIS ENTIRE LIFE.
BACON. THAT WOULD BE A PERFECT NAME FOR A BAND...AND IT SOUNDS LIKE BAKIN'? YOU KNOW, BAKING? LIKE GETTING BAKED?
...AND YOU THINK ABOUT FRYING BACON AND GETTING FRIED, RIGHT?
ROY AND I WERE TALKING ABOUT STARTING A BAND BUT EVERYONE'S GOT A BAND...WE HAVE TO COME UP WITH SOME-THING ELSE... LIKE MAYBE A MAGAZINE OR SOMETHING.
THERE WAS A LOT OF CONFUSION WHEN THE POLICE SHOWED UP, BUT I GUESS HE PUNCHED OUT ONE OF THE COPS.
HE WAS ALREADY ON PROBATION SO THAT WAS ENOUGH TO PUT HIM AWAY FOR A LONG, LONG TIME.
WE SHOULD CHOP UP THE REST OF THIS COKE...THEN WE'LL BE DONE WITH IT. I PROMISED ROY I'D SAVE SOME FOR HIM BUT...BUT HE NEVER SHOWED UP SO FUCK HIM!
VICEROY
I COULD TRY CALLING HIM AGAIN, BUT I DON'T KNOW... HE MAKES ME SO CRAZY! WHY DIDN'T HE COME TO THE PARTY LAST NIGHT? WHERE WAS HE?
GO AHEAD AND CALL HIM, I'LL BET HE'S HOME BY NOW.
I COULDN'T REALLY FIGURE OUT IF SARAH WAS RELIEVED OR WHAT...
...BUT I KEPT THINKING TO MYSELF, "HE'S GONE... THIS IS MY CHANCE."

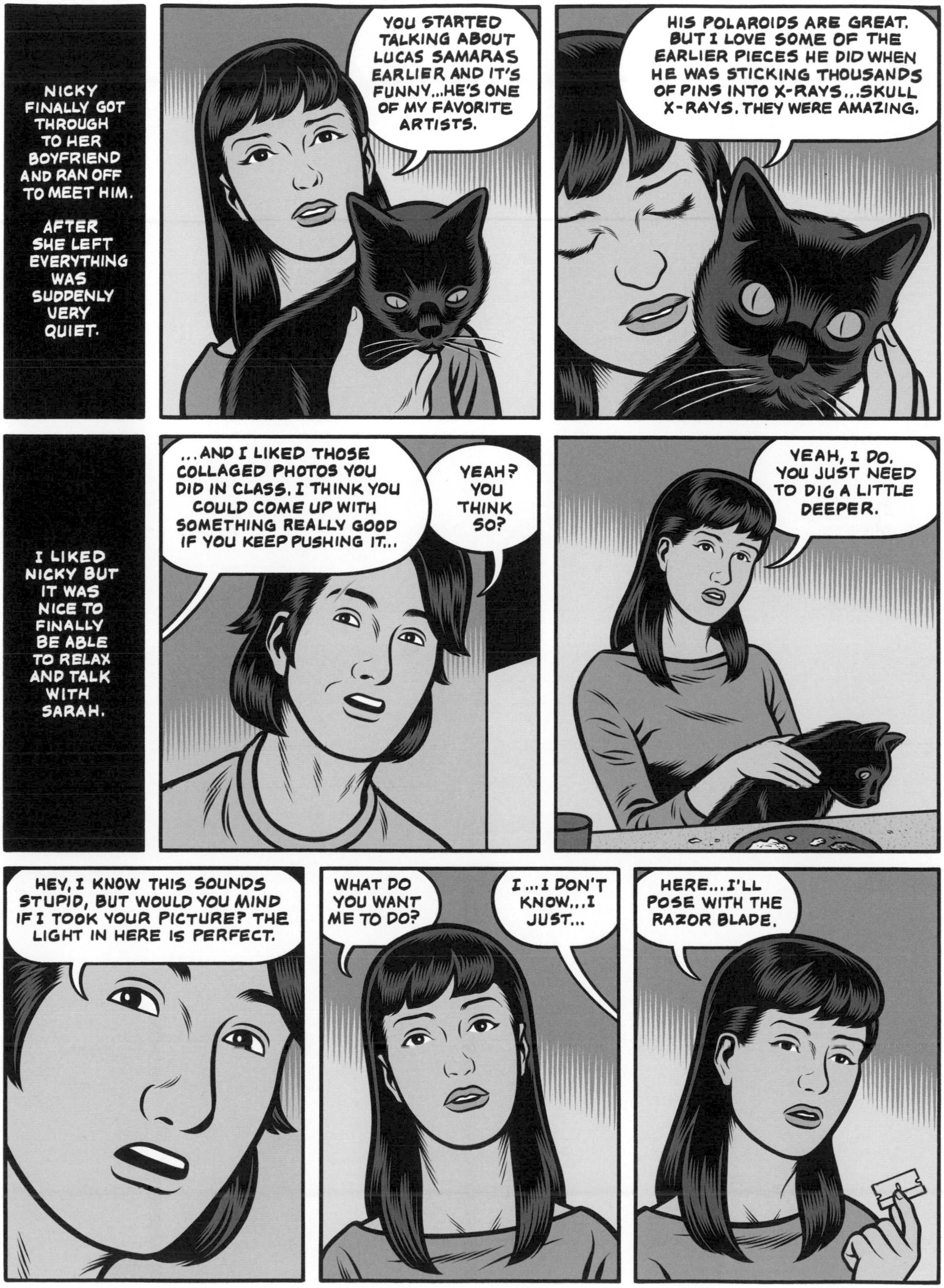
NICKY FINALLY GOT THROUGH TO HER BOYFRIEND AND RAN OFF TO MEET HIM.
AFTER SHE LEFT EVERYTHING WAS SUDDENLY VERY QUIET.
YOU STARTED TALKING ABOUT LUCAS SAMARAS EARLIER AND IT'S FUNNY...HE'S ONE OF MY FAVORITE ARTISTS.
HIS POLAROIDS ARE GREAT. BUT I LOVE SOME OF THE EARLIER PIECES HE DID WHEN HE WAS STICKING THOUSANDS OF PINS INTO X-RAYS...SKULL X-RAYS. THEY WERE AMAZING.
I LIKED NICKY BUT IT WAS NICE TO FINALLY BE ABLE TO RELAX AND TALK WITH SARAH.
...AND I LIKED THOSE COLLAGED PHOTOS YOU DID IN CLASS. I THINK YOU COULD COME UP WITH SOMETHING REALLY GOOD IF YOU KEEP PUSHING IT...
YEAH? YOU THINK SO?
YEAH, I DO. YOU JUST NEED TO DIG A LITTLE DEEPER.
HEY, I KNOW THIS SOUNDS STUPID, BUT WOULD YOU MIND IF I TOOK YOUR PICTURE? THE LIGHT IN HERE IS PERFECT.
WHAT DO YOU WANT ME TO DO?
I...I DON'T KNOW...I JUST...
HERE...I'LL POSE WITH THE RAZOR BLADE.

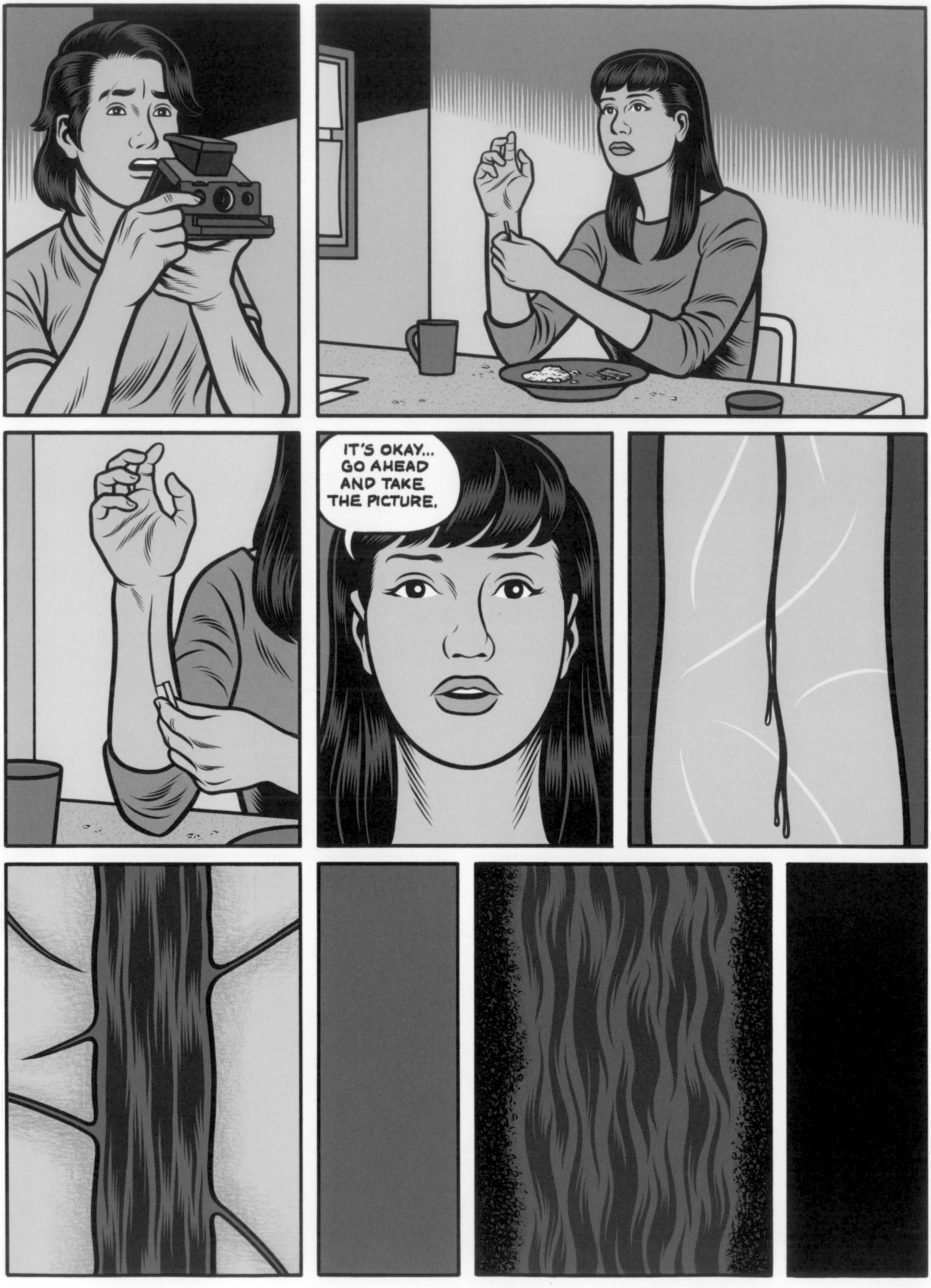
IT'S OKAY... GO AHEAD AND TAKE THE PICTURE.

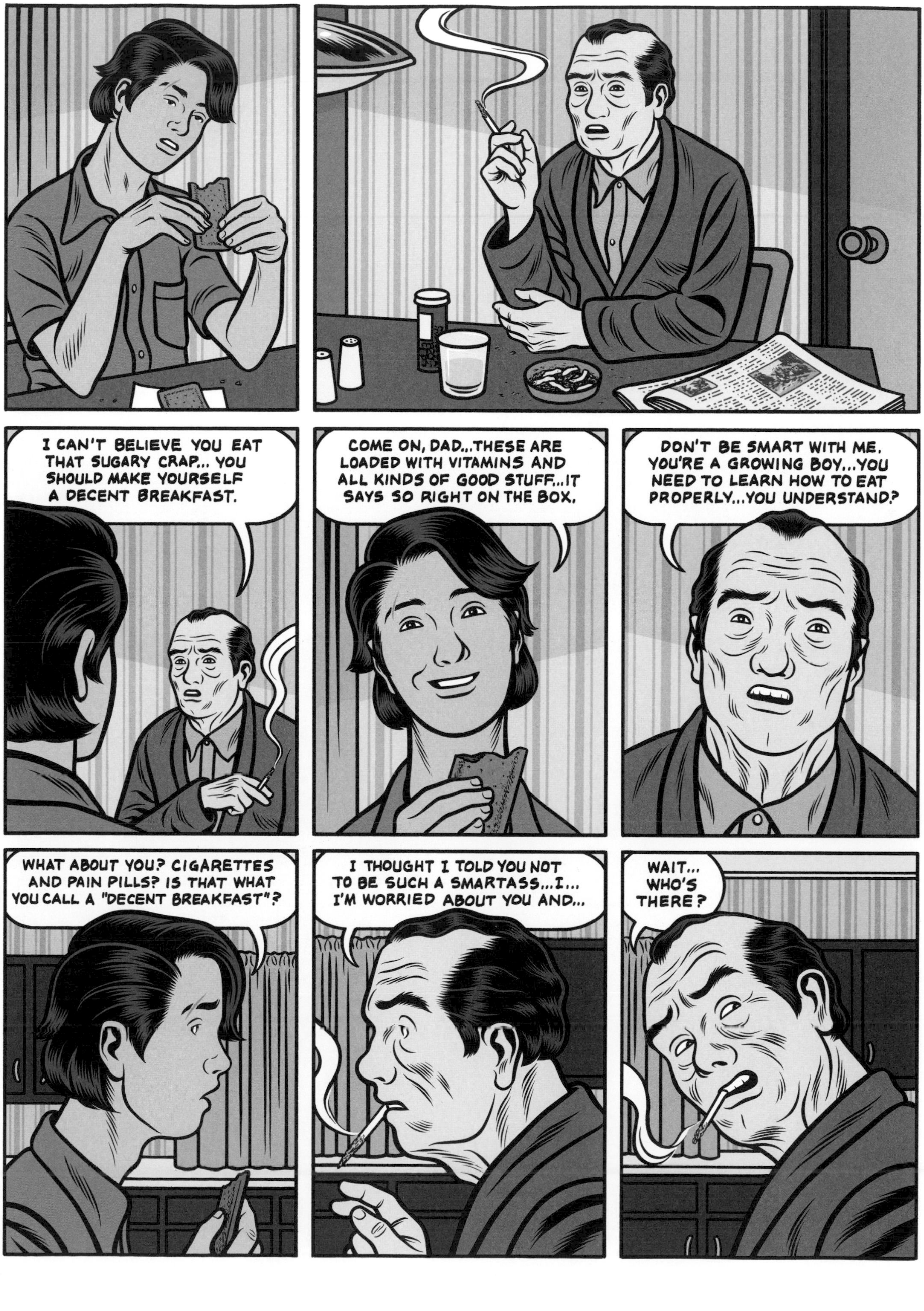
I CAN'T BELIEVE YOU EAT THAT SUGARY CRAP... YOU SHOULD MAKE YOURSELF A DECENT BREAKFAST.
COME ON, DAD...THESE ARE LOADED WITH VITAMINS AND ALL KINDS OF GOOD STUFF...IT SAYS SO RIGHT ON THE BOX.
DON'T BE SMART WITH ME. YOU'RE A GROWING BOY...YOU NEED TO LEARN HOW TO EAT PROPERLY...YOU UNDERSTAND?
WHAT ABOUT YOU? CIGARETTES AND PAIN PILLS? IS THAT WHAT YOU CALL A "DECENT BREAKFAST"?
I THOUGHT I TOLD YOU NOT TO BE SUCH A SMARTASS...I... I'M WORRIED ABOUT YOU AND...
WAIT... WHO'S THERE?

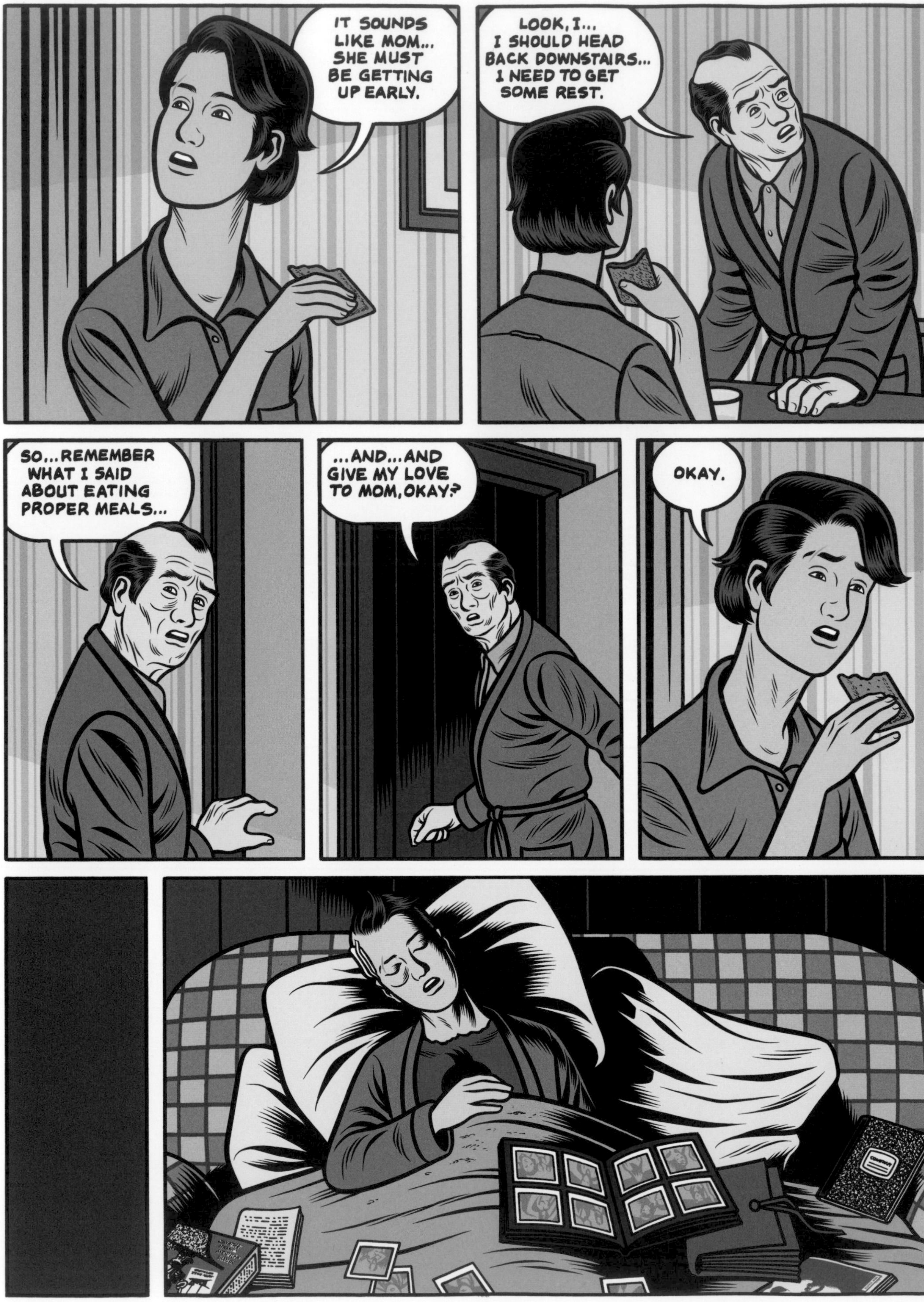
IT SOUNDS LIKE MOM... SHE MUST BE GETTING UP EARLY.
LOOK, I... I SHOULD HEAD BACK DOWNSTAIRS... I NEED TO GET SOME REST.
SO... REMEMBER WHAT I SAID ABOUT EATING PROPER MEALS...
...AND... AND GIVE MY LOVE TO MOM, OKAY?
OKAY.

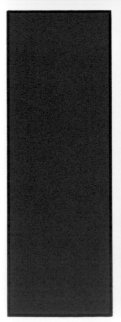

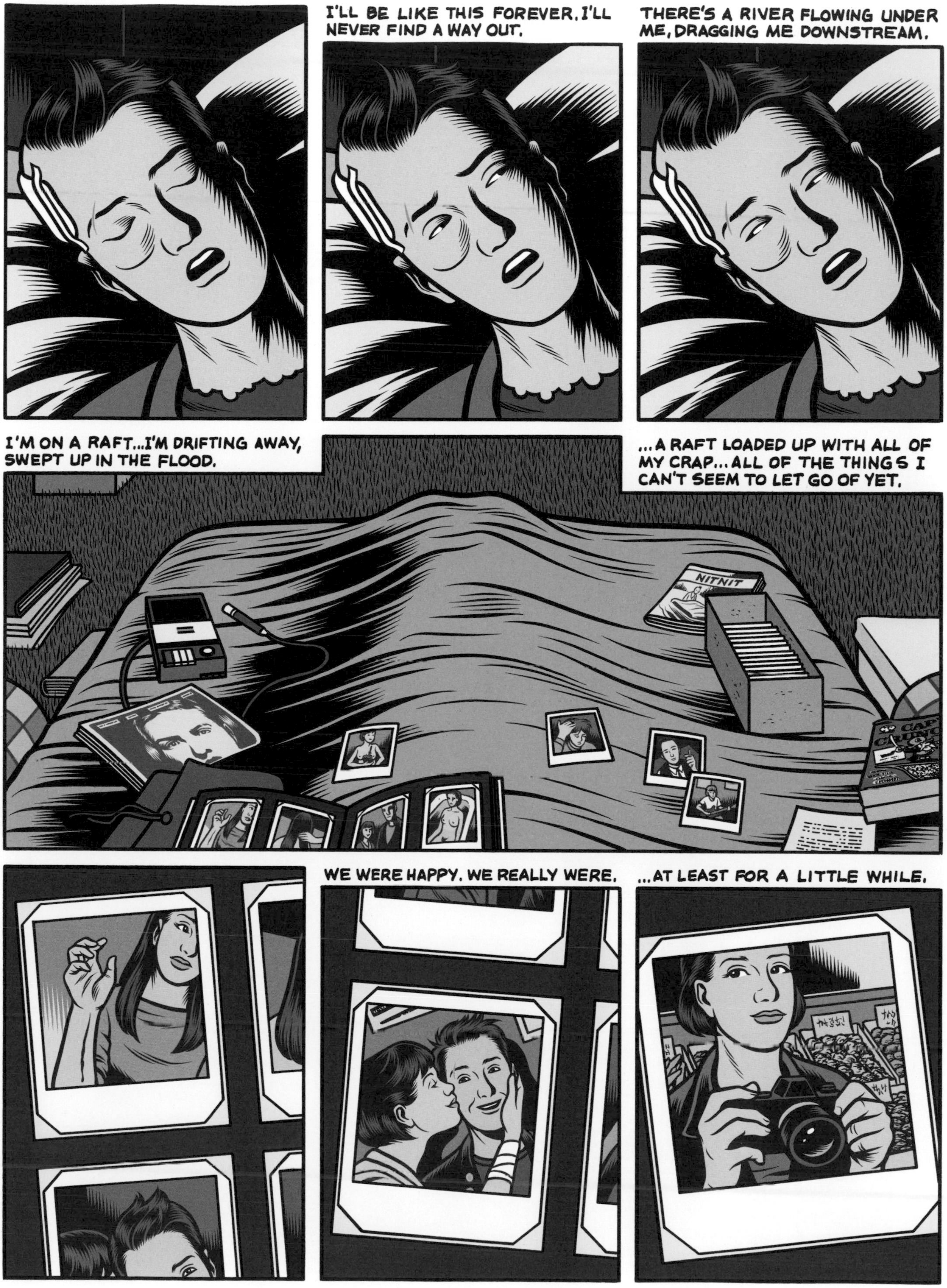
I'LL BE LIKE THIS FOREVER. I'LL NEVER FIND A WAY OUT.
THERE'S A RIVER FLOWING UNDER ME, DRAGGING ME DOWNSTREAM.
I'M ON A RAFT...I'M DRIFTING AWAY, SWEPT UP IN THE FLOOD.
...A RAFT LOADED UP WITH ALL OF MY CRAP... ALL OF THE THINGS I CAN'T SEEM TO LET GO OF YET.
NITNIT
WE WERE HAPPY. WE REALLY WERE.
...AT LEAST FOR A LITTLE WHILE.

...WAKING UP WITH SARAH ON A CLEAR, BEAUTIFUL DAY,

WALKING WITH HER THROUGH CHINATOWN, THE SKY IMPOSSIBLY BRIGHT AND BLUE.

I TRY TO CONTROL IT...

TRY TO FOCUS IN ON THE GOOD THINGS.

EVERYTHING BRIGHT AND CLEAN AND NEW.

...BUT MY EYES ALWAYS DRIFT...

I ALWAYS LOOK DOWN.

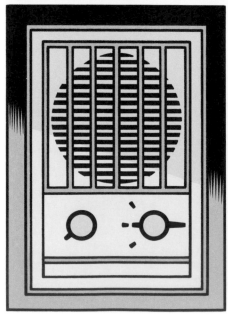

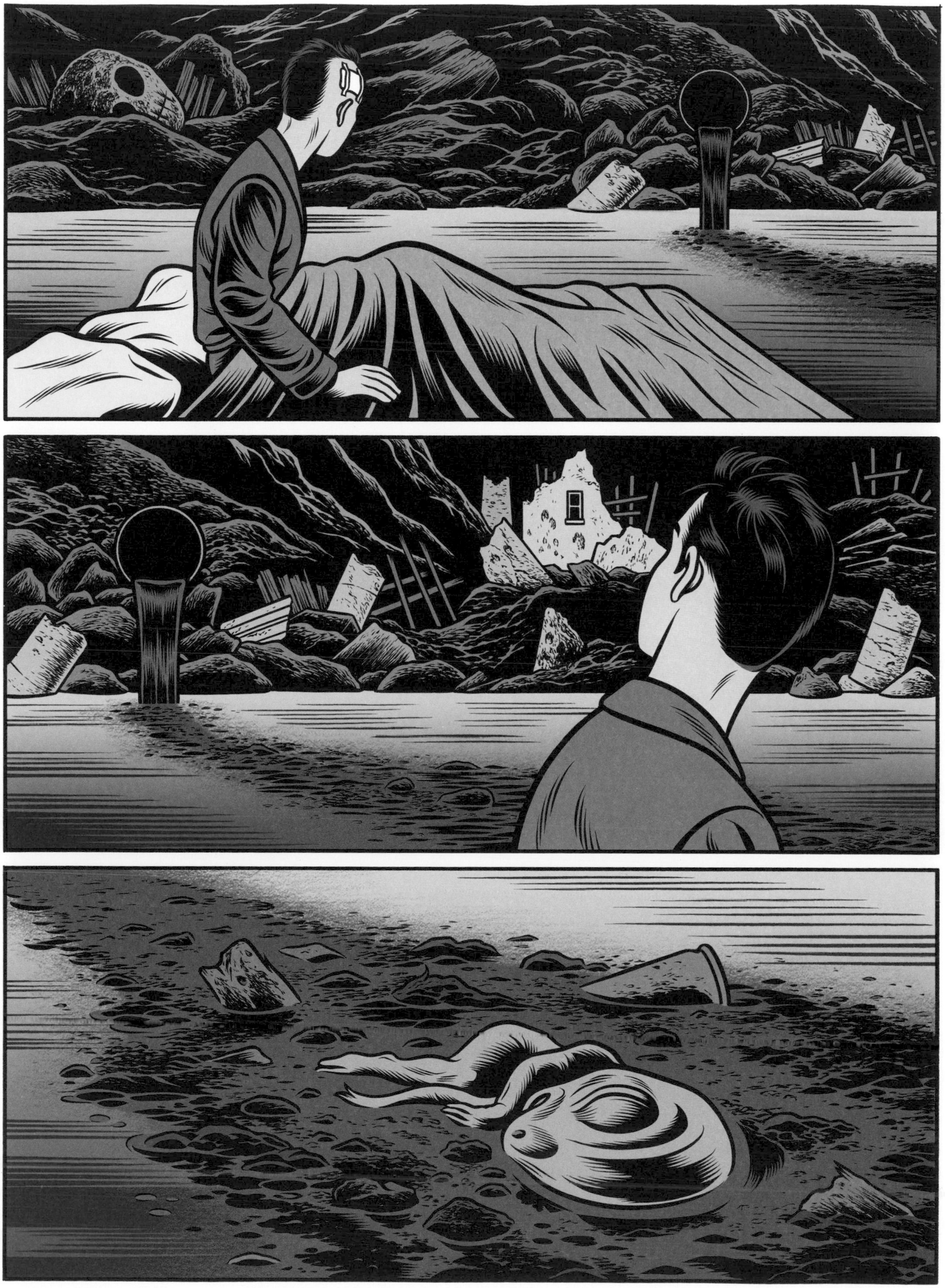

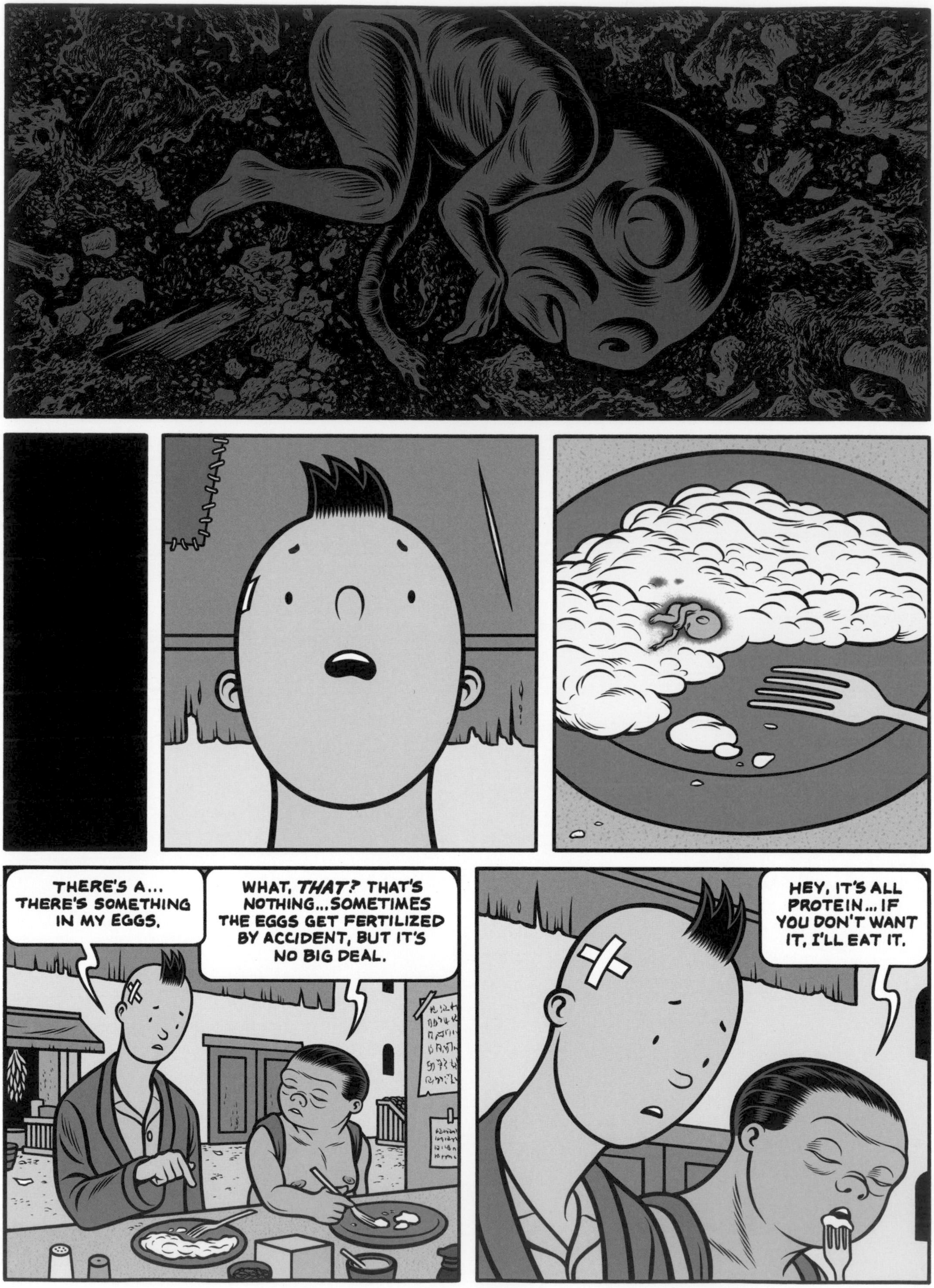
THERE'S A... THERE'S SOMETHING IN MY EGGS.
WHAT, *THAT?* THAT'S NOTHING... SOMETIMES THE EGGS GET FERTILIZED BY ACCIDENT, BUT IT'S NO BIG DEAL.
HEY, IT'S ALL PROTEIN... IF YOU DON'T WANT IT, I'LL EAT IT.

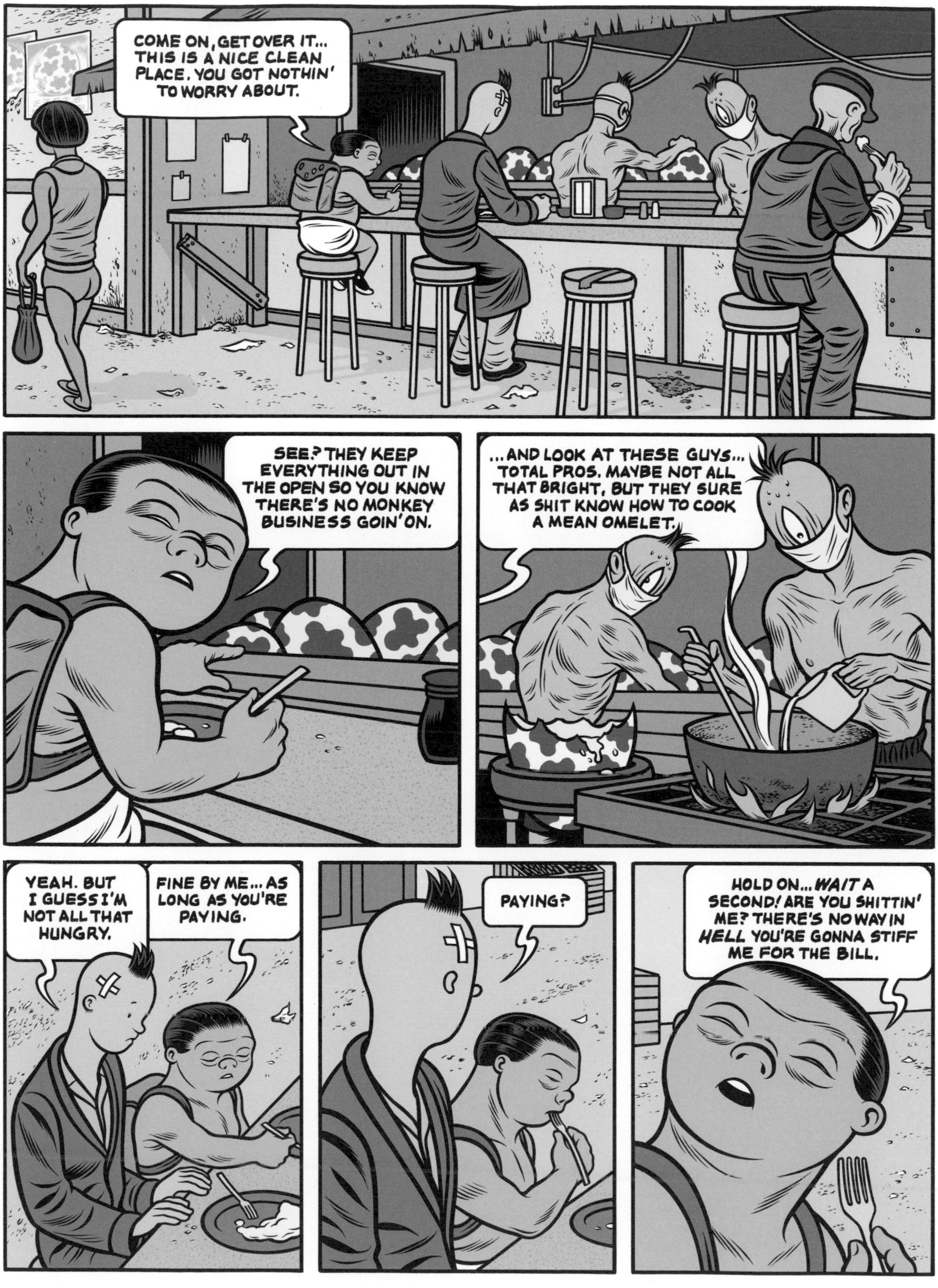
COME ON, GET OVER IT... THIS IS A NICE CLEAN PLACE. YOU GOT NOTHIN' TO WORRY ABOUT.
SEE? THEY KEEP EVERYTHING OUT IN THE OPEN SO YOU KNOW THERE'S NO MONKEY BUSINESS GOIN' ON.
...AND LOOK AT THESE GUYS... TOTAL PROS. MAYBE NOT ALL THAT BRIGHT, BUT THEY SURE AS SHIT KNOW HOW TO COOK A MEAN OMELET.
YEAH. BUT I GUESS I'M NOT ALL THAT HUNGRY.
FINE BY ME... AS LONG AS YOU'RE PAYING.
PAYING?
HOLD ON... WAIT A SECOND! ARE YOU SHITTIN' ME? THERE'S NO WAY IN HELL YOU'RE GONNA STIFF ME FOR THE BILL.

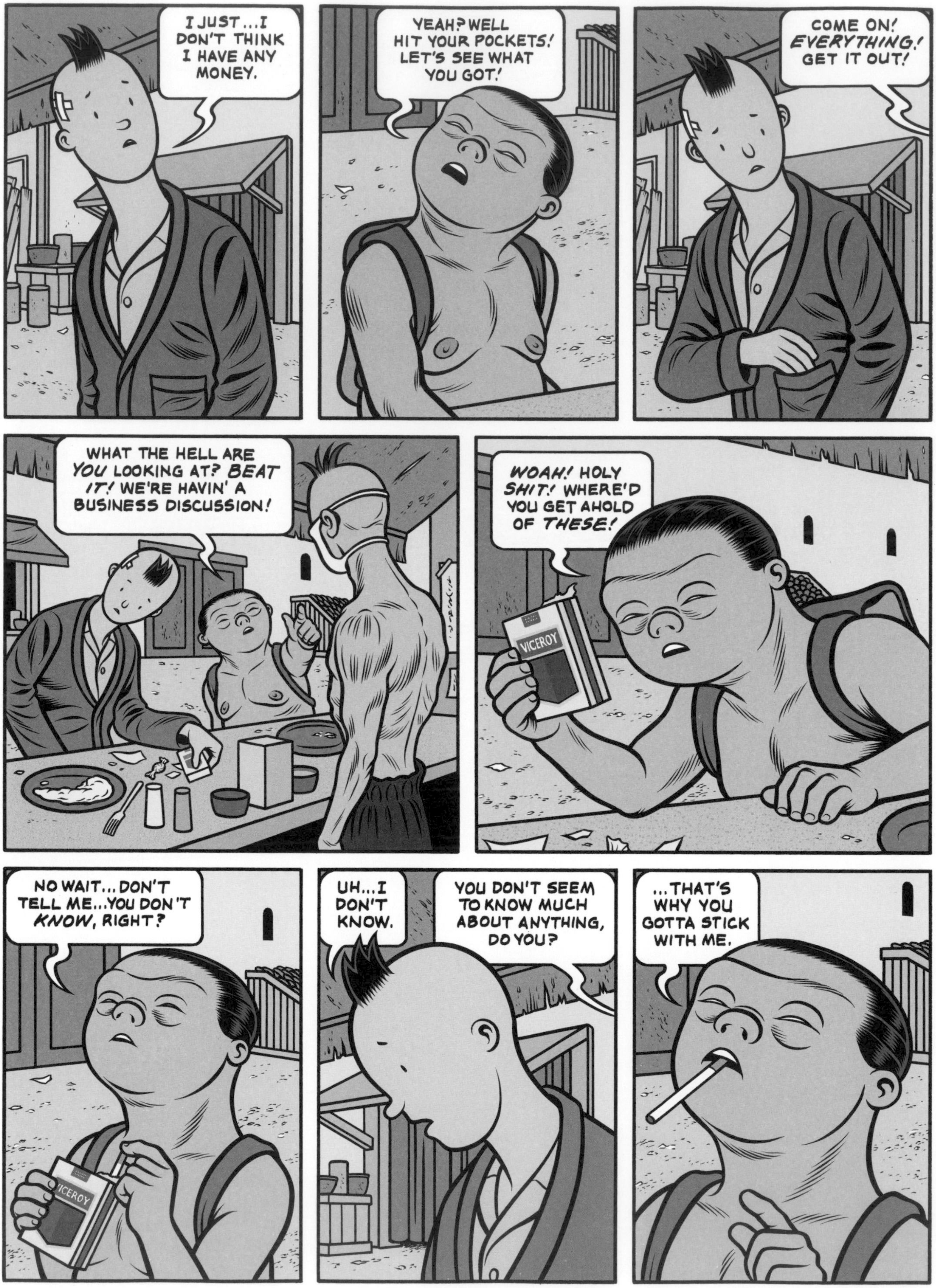
I JUST...I DON'T THINK I HAVE ANY MONEY.
YEAH? WELL HIT YOUR POCKETS! LET'S SEE WHAT YOU GOT!
COME ON! EVERYTHING! GET IT OUT!
WHAT THE HELL ARE YOU LOOKING AT? BEAT IT! WE'RE HAVIN' A BUSINESS DISCUSSION!
WOAH! HOLY SHIT! WHERE'D YOU GET AHOLD OF THESE!
VICEROY
NO WAIT... DON'T TELL ME...YOU DON'T KNOW, RIGHT?
VICEROY
UH...I DON'T KNOW.
YOU DON'T SEEM TO KNOW MUCH ABOUT ANYTHING, DO YOU?
...THAT'S WHY YOU GOTTA STICK WITH ME.

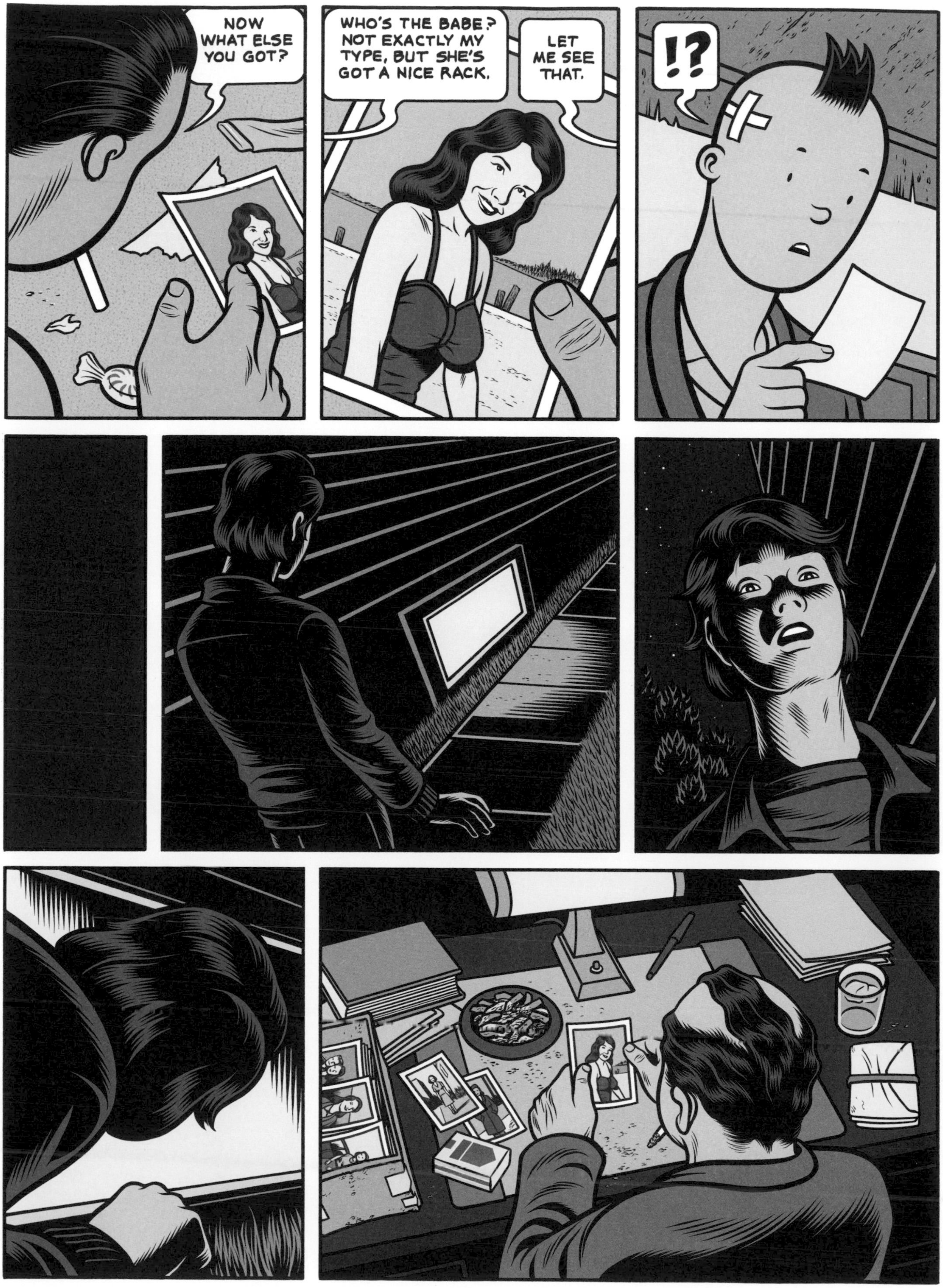
NOW WHAT ELSE YOU GOT?
WHO'S THE BABE? NOT EXACTLY MY TYPE, BUT SHE'S GOT A NICE RACK.
LET ME SEE THAT.
!?

OKAY, PAY ATTENTION... I WANT YOU TO WATCH A *MASTER* AT WORK!

HEY, GARÇON! TIME TO SETTLE UP!

LOOK! ONE CIGGIE, TWO PLATES... YOU SAVVY?

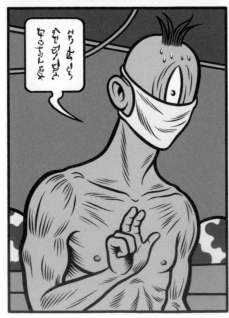

FUCK THAT NOISE! ONE CIGGIE AND THAT'S IT! THIS HERE'S TOP NOTCH, YOU DIG?

SEE? NO PROBLEM. YOU JUST HAVE TO KNOW HOW TO BARGAIN WITH THESE GUYS.

SO LISTEN, THESE SMOKES WILL HELP PAY OUR WAY FOR A LITTLE WHILE, BUT THEY WON'T LAST FOREVER.
WE GOTTA THINK ABOUT YOUR FUTURE... FIND YOU A CRIB AND SOME KINDA JOB, RIGHT?
HEY! MOVE IT!
!!
YOU DEAF? GET YOUR ASS OUTTA THE WAY!
DUMB SHIT!
HUH... I GUESS THEY FOUND A NEW QUEEN.

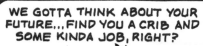

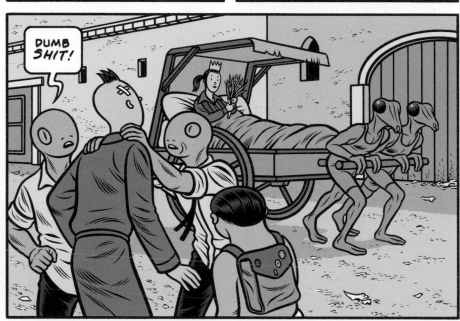

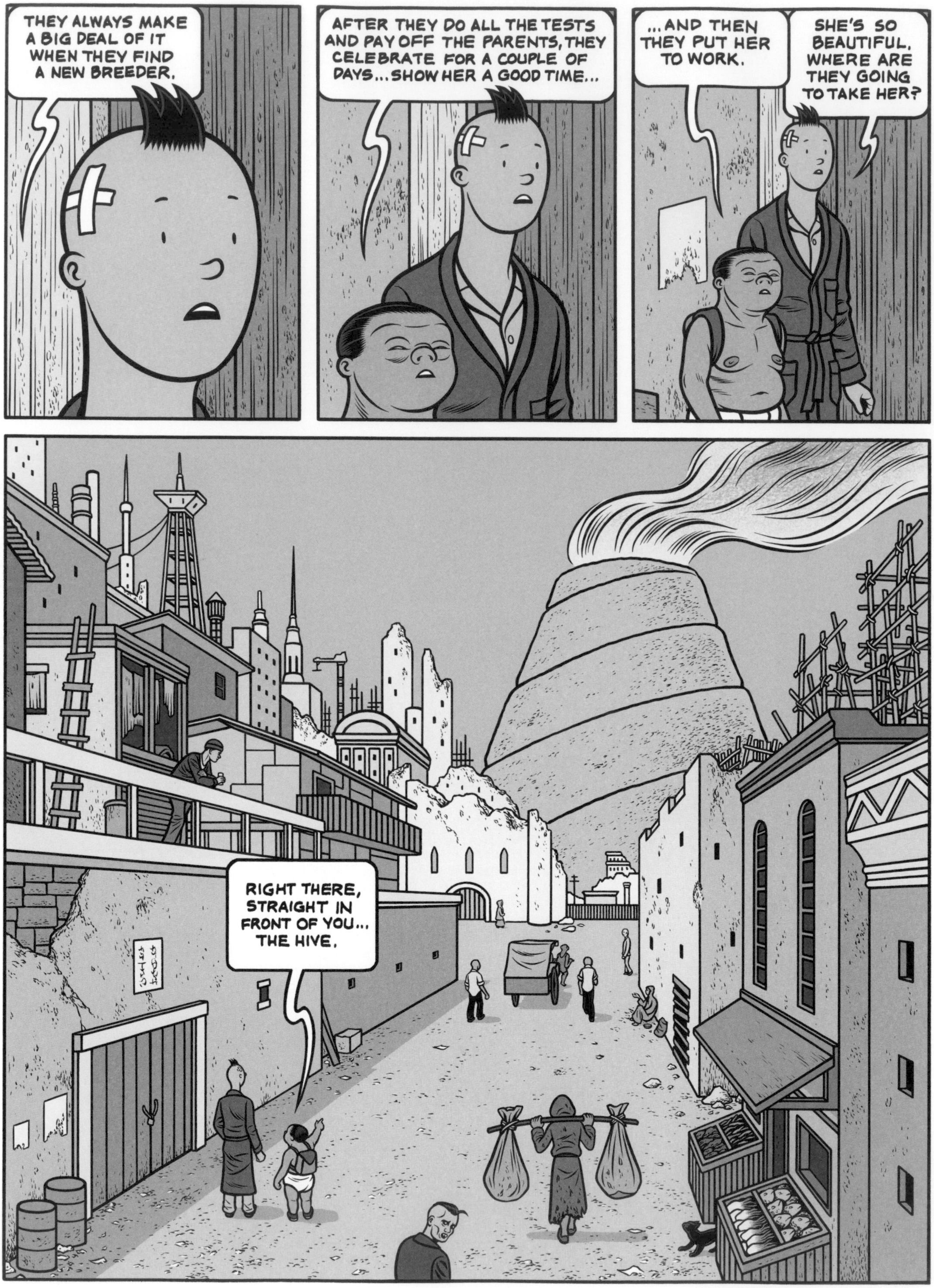
THEY ALWAYS MAKE A BIG DEAL OF IT WHEN THEY FIND A NEW BREEDER.
AFTER THEY DO ALL THE TESTS AND PAY OFF THE PARENTS, THEY CELEBRATE FOR A COUPLE OF DAYS... SHOW HER A GOOD TIME...
...AND THEN THEY PUT HER TO WORK.
SHE'S SO BEAUTIFUL. WHERE ARE THEY GOING TO TAKE HER?
RIGHT THERE, STRAIGHT IN FRONT OF YOU... THE HIVE.

NEXT: THE HIVE

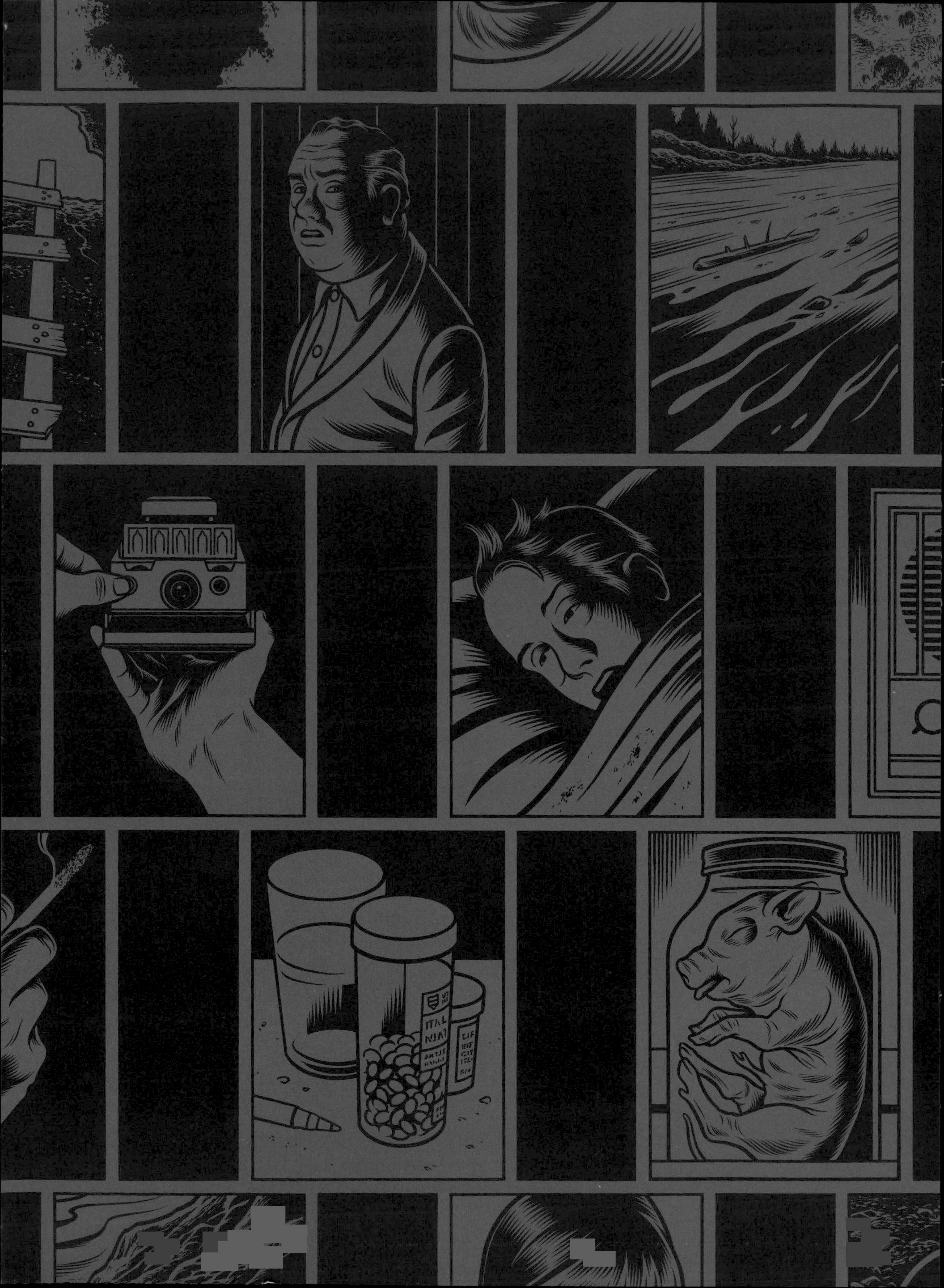